Micro
Habits

Micro Habits
Small Changes, Big Impact

Walter Smith

Published by
Rupa Publications India Pvt. Ltd 2024
7/16, Ansari Road, Daryaganj
New Delhi 110002

Sales centres:
Bengaluru Chennai
Hyderabad Jaipur Kathmandu
Kolkata Mumbai Prayagraj

Copyright © Rupa Publications India Pvt. Ltd 2024

The views and opinions expressed in this book are the author's own and the facts are as reported by him which have been verified to the extent possible, and the publishers are not in any way liable for the same.

All rights reserved.
No part of this publication may be reproduced, transmitted, or stored in a retrieval system, in any form or by any means, electronic, mechanical, photocopying, recording or otherwise, without the prior permission of the publisher.

P-ISBN: 978-93-6156-757-5
E-ISBN: 978-93-6156-078-1

First impression 2024

10 9 8 7 6 5 4 3 2 1

The moral right of the author has been asserted.

This book is sold subject to the condition that it shall not, by way of trade or otherwise, be lent, resold, hired out, or otherwise circulated, without the publisher's prior consent, in any form of binding or cover other than that in which it is published.

Contents

1. Introduction — 1
2. The Ripple Effect of Habits: How Good and Bad Habits Shape Your Life — 11
3. The Journey of Habits: From Formation to Automation — 19
4. Building New Habits Upon Old Ones: The Power of Habit Stacking — 29
5. How Our Environment Shapes Our Habits — 37
6. The Power of Self-Control: Mastering Habits for a Better Life — 53
7. Developing Irresistible Habits: The Science of Dopamine and Motivation — 65
8. A Society of Habits: The Influence of Family, Friends and Celebrities on Habit Formation — 73
9. Find and Fix: Bad Habits and How to Overcome Them — 82
10. Repeat, Repeat, Repeat: The Power of Discipline in Habit Formation — 91
11. Stop That Procrastination: Forming Habits One Step at a Time — 101
12. Say Hello to Good Habits and Bye-Bye to Bad Habits — 112

13. How to Make Any Habits Rewarding
    and Satisfying   119
14. How to Keep Your Habits on Track
    and Bounce Back Quickly   128
15. Breaking the Cycle: Ensuring Bad Habits
    Don't Return   138
16. Your Perfect Habit Match: What Your Genes
    and Personality Says   150
17. Beating Boredom: Staying Motivated and
    Fascinated with Good Habits   165
18. Flexibility Over Rigidity: Adapting Habits
    with Changing Times   177
19. Staying Motivated: How to Bounce Back When
    You Slip Up on Your Habits   187
20. The Journey to Lasting Change: Building
    Small Habits for a Lifetime   198
21. To Establish New Routines, Learn to
    Embrace Setbacks   210
22. Interactive Exercises for Forming Good Habits   214

1

Introduction

In today's fast-paced world, we often seek immediate results and instant gratification. The allure of drastic transformations and quick fixes can overshadow the importance of small, consistent actions. However, the concept of atomic habits—tiny, seemingly insignificant actions that compound over time—holds the key to achieving lasting success and profound personal growth. This chapter explores the science behind atomic habits, delves into their transformative power, and provides practical strategies and real-life examples to help you harness their potential for meaningful change.

The Science Behind Micro and Small Habits

Micro habits are rooted in the principles of behavioural science. Our brains are designed to form habits as a way to conserve energy and streamline daily tasks. When an action is repeated consistently, it becomes automatic, freeing up mental resources for more complex activities. This process, known as automaticity, is the foundation of habit formation. The neurological basis for habit formation lies in the basal ganglia, a region of the brain associated with the development of habits and routines. When we perform an action repeatedly, neural pathways are strengthened, making the behaviour more automatic. This is why habits, once formed, require less conscious effort to execute. Consider the example of brushing your teeth. This routine action doesn't require much thought because it has become ingrained in your daily routine. The same principle applies to other habits, whether it's exercising, reading or practicing mindfulness. By focusing on small, manageable changes, you can leverage the brain's natural tendency to automate behaviours, leading to lasting transformation.

The Power of Small Changes

1. **Compound Effect:** The most compelling aspect of atomic habits is the compound effect. Just as compound interest can lead to significant financial growth over time, small habits can accumulate to create substantial personal and professional improvements. The compound effect is the principle that small, consistent actions, when repeated over time, lead to significant outcomes. Imagine a scenario where you aim to improve your fitness by walking for just 10 minutes a day. Initially, this may seem trivial, but over a year, it translates to more than 60 hours of walking. This cumulative effect can result in weight loss, improved cardiovascular health and increased overall well-being. The key is consistency; each small action builds upon the previous one, creating a powerful momentum that drives progress.
2. **Sustainability:** Large, drastic changes can be overwhelming and difficult to sustain. In contrast, small habits are more manageable and less intimidating, making them easier to integrate into your daily routine. This sustainability is crucial for long-term success. For instance, committing to a five-minute daily meditation practice is more feasible than trying to meditate for an hour every day from the start.

Sustainable habits are those that can be maintained over the long-term without causing burnout or excessive strain. When you set small, achievable goals, you create a foundation for consistent progress. This approach ensures that you don't become discouraged by setbacks or overwhelmed by the magnitude of your goals. Instead, you build a steady, sustainable path towards your desired outcome.

3. **Momentum and Motivation:** Achieving small wins boosts motivation and builds momentum. Each small success reinforces your belief in your ability to change, creating a positive feedback loop. Consider the example of starting a fitness routine. By beginning with a simple goal, such as a 10-minute walk each day, you build confidence and set the stage for more ambitious fitness goals in the future. Momentum is a powerful force that propels you forward. When you experience success with small habits, it creates a sense of accomplishment and encourages you to continue. This momentum can be harnessed to tackle more challenging tasks and goals, leading to a cycle of continuous improvement. The key is to focus on the process rather than the outcome, celebrating each small step along the way.

Strategies for Building Micro Habits

1. **Start Small and Be Specific:** One of the fundamental principles of atomic habits is to start small and be specific. Define clear, specific actions that are easy to accomplish. Instead of setting a vague goal like "exercise more," specify the action, such as "do 10 push-ups every morning." By breaking down your goals into manageable tasks, you increase the likelihood of success. For example, if your goal is to improve your diet, start with a small, specific habit

like drinking a glass of water before each meal. This simple action can lead to improved hydration, better digestion and a reduced likelihood of overeating. Over time, you can build on this habit by incorporating additional healthy behaviours, such as eating more vegetables or reducing sugar intake.

2. **Make It Obvious:** Increase the visibility of your desired habit. Our environment plays a significant role in shaping our behaviour, and making your habit cues obvious can help reinforce the desired action. For instance, if you want to eat more fruits, place a bowl of fresh fruit on your kitchen counter where you can see it easily. This visual cue serves as a reminder to choose a healthy snack. Another example is placing your workout clothes and shoes by your bed before sleeping. When you wake up, the sight of your workout gear will prompt you to exercise. By making your cues obvious, you reduce the need for willpower and make it easier to initiate the desired behaviour.

3. **Make It Attractive:** Pair your desired habit with an activity you enjoy. Our brains are wired to seek pleasure and avoid pain, so making your habit attractive increases the likelihood of adherence. For example, if you want to build a reading habit, read a chapter of your favourite book while enjoying a cup of your favourite tea. By associating the habit with something pleasurable, you create a positive experience that encourages repetition. Another approach is to use a technique called "temptation bundling," where you pair a habit you need to do with a habit you want to do. For instance, if you enjoy watching your favourite TV show, only allow yourself to watch it while you exercise on a stationary bike. This way, you create a positive association with the habit, making it more appealing and enjoyable.

4. **Make It Easy:** Reduce the friction that makes it hard to

perform the habit. The easier a habit is to perform, the more likely you are to do it consistently. Lay out your workout clothes the night before to make it easier to exercise in the morning. Simplify the process by removing obstacles and minimizing the effort required to initiate the habit. For example, if you want to develop a writing habit, keep a notebook and pen on your bedside table. This way, you can easily jot down your thoughts or ideas before going to sleep or upon waking up. By making the habit easy and accessible, you increase the likelihood of incorporating it into your daily routine.

5. **Make It Satisfying:** Incorporate immediate rewards to reinforce the habit. Use a habit tracker to mark your progress, which gives you a visual reminder of your achievements. This sense of accomplishment and satisfaction reinforces the behaviour and motivates you to continue. Positive reinforcement is a powerful tool in habit formation, and by making your habits satisfying, you create a positive feedback loop. For example, if you want to build a habit of saving money, reward yourself with a small treat or experience each time you reach a savings milestone. This immediate gratification reinforces the habit and encourages you to continue saving. The key is to choose rewards that align with your values and goals, ensuring that they enhance rather than undermine your progress.

Real-Life Examples and Anecdotes

1. **The Story of Jerry Seinfeld:** The famous comedian Jerry Seinfeld used a simple strategy to maintain his writing habit. He hung a large calendar on his wall and made a mark on each day he wrote jokes. His goal was to keep the streak going, and the visual representation of his progress motivated

him to write consistently. This "don't break the chain" method is a powerful way to build and sustain micro habits. Seinfeld's approach highlights the importance of tracking progress and maintaining consistency. By focusing on the process rather than the outcome, he was able to develop a sustainable writing habit that contributed to his success. The visual reminder of his streak provided immediate feedback and reinforced his commitment to daily writing.

2. **The Power of 1% Improvements:** British cycling coach Dave Brailsford employed the principle of marginal gains to transform British Cycling into a world-dominating force. By focusing on 1% improvements in various areas—nutrition, equipment, training techniques—Brailsford's team achieved remarkable success, including multiple Tour de France victories and Olympic gold medals. This approach underscores the profound impact of small, incremental changes. Brailsford's strategy involved breaking down the components of cycling performance and seeking small improvements in each area. These marginal gains, when combined, led to significant overall performance enhancements. The principle of 1% improvements can be applied to various aspects of life, demonstrating that small changes, when compounded over time, lead to substantial results.

3. **Personal Finance Success:** Consider the example of someone trying to save money. Instead of attempting to save large sums sporadically, they commit to saving just $5 a day. Over a year, this small habit results in savings of $1,825. The key is consistency, demonstrating that even modest efforts can yield significant financial gains over time. This approach to saving emphasizes the power of small, consistent actions in achieving financial goals. By breaking down the goal into manageable daily habits, you create a sustainable path to

financial stability. The principle of atomic habits applies to personal finance, highlighting the importance of consistent, incremental savings.

4. **Health and Fitness Transformation:** James Clear, the author of *Atomic Habits*, shares his personal experience of using small habits to recover from a severe injury. By starting with simple, manageable exercises and gradually increasing their intensity, he was able to rebuild his strength and transform his health. His journey exemplifies the power of atomic habits in achieving long-term fitness goals. Clear's approach involved focusing on small, achievable actions that could be performed consistently. By starting with basic exercises and gradually increasing the difficulty, he created a sustainable fitness routine. This method highlights the importance of patience and persistence in achieving health and fitness goals, demonstrating that small habits can lead to significant transformations.

Overcoming Challenges and Staying on Track

1. **Habit Stacking:** Link your new habit to an existing one to create a seamless routine. Habit stacking involves using an established habit as a cue for the new habit you want to build. For example, if you want to practise gratitude, do it right after brushing your teeth each morning. This approach leverages the consistency of an existing habit to reinforce the new behaviour. Habit stacking is effective because it reduces the need for additional willpower and creates a natural flow in your daily routine. By anchoring your new habit to an existing one, you increase the likelihood of consistency and make it easier to integrate the new behaviour into your life.
2. **Environment Design:** Shape your environment to support

your habits. Our surroundings have a significant impact on our behaviour, and by designing your environment to reinforce your desired habits, you can increase the likelihood of success. Remove distractions and obstacles that hinder your progress. If you want to reduce screen time, keep your phone out of the bedroom. For example, if you want to develop a habit of healthy eating, stock your kitchen with nutritious foods and remove unhealthy snacks. Arrange your environment to make the healthy choice the easy choice. By creating a supportive environment, you reduce the friction and resistance that can impede your progress.

3. **Accountability and Support:** Share your goals with a friend or join a community with similar aspirations. Accountability partners can provide encouragement and help you stay committed. Social support is a powerful motivator, and having someone to share your journey with can make the process more enjoyable and rewarding. For example, if you want to develop a regular exercise routine, find a workout buddy or join a fitness group. The social connection and shared commitment create a sense of accountability and motivation. Additionally, celebrating your successes with others can enhance your sense of accomplishment and reinforce your habits.

4. **Embrace the Process:** Focus on the journey rather than the destination. Celebrate small victories and view setbacks as opportunities for learning and growth. The goal is consistent progress, not perfection. Embracing the process means acknowledging that change takes time and effort, and that setbacks are a natural part of the journey. For example, if you're working on a writing habit, don't get discouraged by occasional writer's block or missed writing sessions. Instead, celebrate the days you do write and use

setbacks as opportunities to reflect and adjust your approach. By focusing on the process, you cultivate resilience and persistence, essential qualities for long-term success.

Conclusion

Atomic habits hold the key to unlocking your full potential. By embracing the power of small changes, you can create lasting, meaningful transformations in every area of your life. Whether it's improving your health, building a successful career or enhancing personal relationships, the principles of atomic habits provide a practical framework for achieving your goals. Start today by identifying one small habit you can integrate into your routine, and watch as these incremental changes compound over time, leading to extraordinary results.

Remember, the journey of a thousand miles begins with a single step. Embrace the power of atomic habits and take that first step towards a brighter, more fulfilling future. The path to success is not defined by grand gestures but by the consistent application of small, intentional actions. By focusing on the process and celebrating each small victory, you build a foundation for lasting change and unlock the potential for continuous growth and improvement.

Practical Exercises

1. **Habit Tracker:** Create a simple habit tracker to monitor your progress. List your desired habits and mark each day you successfully complete them. This visual tool reinforces consistency and provides a sense of accomplishment. A habit tracker can be as simple as a calendar or a dedicated app that helps you stay accountable and motivated.

2. **Reflection Journal:** Maintain a reflection journal to document your experiences, challenges and insights as you work on building atomic habits. Reflecting on your journey helps you stay mindful and make necessary adjustments. Writing about your progress and setbacks allows you to gain perspective and identify patterns that can inform your approach to habit formation.
3. **Accountability Partner:** Find an accountability partner who shares similar goals. Schedule regular check-ins to discuss your progress, share tips and provide mutual support. Having someone to share your journey with creates a sense of responsibility and motivation, making it easier to stay committed to your habits.
4. **Environment Audit:** Conduct an audit of your environment to identify factors that support or hinder your habits. Make necessary changes to create a conducive environment for your desired behaviours. For example, if you want to develop a habit of reading, create a comfortable reading nook in your home and eliminate distractions that may interfere with your reading time.
5. **Mindfulness Practice:** Incorporate mindfulness practices into your daily routine to stay present and aware of your habits. Mindfulness enhances self-awareness and helps you stay focused on your goals. Techniques such as meditation, deep breathing and mindful observation can help you stay grounded and connected to your intentions, making it easier to cultivate and sustain micro habits. By integrating these practical exercises into your daily life, you can create a supportive framework for building and sustaining micro habits. Remember, the key to lasting change lies in the consistent application of small, intentional actions. Embrace the journey, celebrate your progress and trust in the power of atomic habits to transform your life.

2

The Ripple Effect of Habits: How Good and Bad Habits Shape Your Life

Have you ever noticed how some people seem to breeze through life, achieving their goals with ease, while others struggle to make progress? The secret often lies in their habits. Our daily habits—those little actions we perform almost without thinking—can have a massive impact on our lives. Good habits propel us forward, while bad habits hold us back. In this chapter, we'll explore the power of habits, using real-life examples and anecdotes to illustrate how they shape our lives. We'll also dive into practical strategies for cultivating good habits and breaking bad ones.

The Power of Habits

Habits are like the autopilot setting on an aeroplane. They guide our behaviour and decisions without requiring much conscious thought. Over time, these small, repetitive actions accumulate, creating a significant impact on our lives. Think of habits as the compound interest of self-improvement—each one might not seem like much on its own, but together, they determine our trajectory.

Good Habits: Building Blocks for Success

Good habits are the cornerstone of a fulfilling and productive life. They help us achieve our goals, maintain our health and improve our relationships. Let's look at some examples of good habits and their impact.

Example 1: The Habit of Exercise

Consider John, a busy marketing executive. A few years ago, John struggled with low energy levels and frequent bouts of stress. He decided to start a simple habit: jogging for 20 minutes every morning. Initially, it was tough to wake up early, but he pushed through the discomfort. Over time, his morning jog became a natural part of his routine. The benefits were profound. John's energy levels soared, his stress decreased, and he found himself more focused and productive at work. This single habit had a ripple effect, improving various aspects of his life. He even inspired his coworkers to join him, creating a healthier and more energetic office environment.

Example 2: The Habit of Reading

Emily, a young entrepreneur, wanted to expand her knowledge and skills. She started a habit of reading for 30 minutes every night before bed. Over the years, she devoured countless books on business, psychology and personal development. This habit not only broadened her knowledge but also sparked creative ideas that she implemented in her business. As a result, Emily's business flourished, and she became a sought-after speaker in her industry. The habit of reading not only enriched her mind but also had a direct impact on her professional success. Emily's story shows how investing a small amount of time daily in a productive habit can lead to significant long-term benefits.

Bad Habits: Obstacles to Success

Just as good habits can propel us forward, bad habits can hold us back. They drain our time, energy and focus, preventing us from reaching our full potential. Here are some examples of bad habits and their detrimental effects.

Example 1: The Habit of Procrastination

Tom, a talented graphic designer, had a habit of procrastinating. He often delayed starting projects until the last minute, which led to rushed work and missed deadlines. This bad habit not only affected his professional reputation but also caused him significant stress and anxiety. Despite his talent, Tom struggled to advance in his career because of his procrastination habit. He realized that he needed to break this cycle to achieve his goals. Tom started by setting small, achievable deadlines for himself and gradually built a habit of tackling tasks promptly. This shift improved his work quality, reduced his stress and opened up new opportunities for career advancement.

Example 2: The Habit of Unhealthy Eating

Sarah, a busy mother of two, had a habit of relying on fast food and sugary snacks for quick meals. This unhealthy eating habit took a toll on her energy levels and overall health. She often felt tired, sluggish and struggled with weight gain. Realizing the impact of her eating habits, Sarah decided to make a change. She started by incorporating small, healthy habits into her routine, such as drinking more water and preparing simple, nutritious meals. Over time, these changes led to significant improvements in her health and energy levels. Sarah's story highlights how bad habits can negatively affect our well-being and how small, positive changes can turn things around.

The Ripple Effect of Habits

The beauty of habits lies in their ripple effect. One good habit can trigger a chain reaction of positive changes, while one bad habit can create a cascade of negative consequences. Understanding this ripple effect can motivate us to cultivate good habits and break bad ones.

Real-Life Anecdote: The Ripple Effect of a Morning Routine

Meet Lisa, a software developer who struggled with feeling overwhelmed and unproductive. She decided to create a morning routine to start her day on a positive note. Her routine included waking up early, meditating for 10 minutes and writing down her top three priorities for the day. This small change had a profound impact on Lisa's life. Her morning routine helped her feel more centered and focused throughout the day. As a result, she became more productive at work, completed her tasks more efficiently and even found time to pursue her hobbies in the evenings. The ripple effect of this simple morning routine transformed her daily life and overall well-being.

Strategies for Cultivating Good Habits

Building good habits requires intention and consistency. Here are some practical strategies to help you cultivate positive habits that can transform your life.

1. **Start Small:** The key to building a new habit is to start small. Choose a habit that is easy to incorporate into your daily routine. For example, if you want to develop a habit of exercising, start with just five minutes of stretching each

morning. As the habit becomes ingrained, you can gradually increase the duration and intensity.
2. **Be Consistent:** Consistency is crucial for habit formation. Commit to performing your chosen habit every day, even if it's just for a few minutes. The more consistent you are, the more likely the habit will stick. Use reminders, such as setting alarms or placing sticky notes in visible locations, to help you stay on track.
3. **Track Your Progress:** Keeping track of your progress can be highly motivating. Use a habit tracker or journal to record your daily efforts. Seeing your progress visually can reinforce your commitment and help you stay accountable.
4. **Find a Trigger:** Identify a specific trigger that prompts you to perform your habit. For example, if you want to develop a habit of flossing, use brushing your teeth as the trigger. By linking your new habit to an existing routine, you create a natural cue that reminds you to take action.
5. **Reward Yourself:** Incorporate immediate rewards to reinforce your new habit. Treat yourself to something enjoyable after completing your habit, such as enjoying a favourite snack or spending a few minutes on a hobby. Positive reinforcement can make the habit more enjoyable and increase your motivation to stick with it.

Strategies for Breaking Bad Habits

Breaking bad habits can be challenging, but it's possible with the right approach. Here are some strategies to help you overcome negative habits and replace them with positive ones.

1. **Identify Triggers:** The first step in breaking a bad habit is to identify the triggers that prompt the behaviour. Pay

attention to the situations, emotions or people that lead you to engage in the habit. Once you identify the triggers, you can develop strategies to avoid or manage them.
2. **Replace the Habit:** Instead of simply trying to eliminate a bad habit, replace it with a positive one. For example, if you have a habit of snacking on junk food when you're stressed, replace it with a healthier alternative, such as going for a walk or practicing deep breathing exercises.
3. **Change Your Environment:** Your environment plays a significant role in shaping your habits. Make changes to your surroundings to support your efforts to break a bad habit. For example, if you want to reduce screen time, remove electronic devices from your bedroom and create a designated space for screen-free activities.
4. **Seek Support:** Enlist the support of friends, family or a support group to help you break a bad habit. Share your goals and progress with them, and ask for their encouragement and accountability. Having a support system can provide motivation and make the process more manageable.
5. **Be Patient and Persistent:** Breaking a bad habit takes time and effort. Be patient with yourself and recognize that setbacks are a natural part of the process. Stay persistent and continue to focus on your goals, even if progress is slow. Celebrate small victories along the way to keep yourself motivated.

Conclusion

Our habits have a profound impact on our lives. Good habits propel us forward, helping us achieve our goals and improve our well-being, while bad habits hold us back and create obstacles to success. By understanding the power of habits and implementing practical strategies to cultivate positive habits and break negative ones, we can shape our lives for the better. Remember, the key to lasting change lies in the small, consistent actions we take every day. Start by identifying one good habit you can incorporate into your routine and one bad habit you want to break. With intention and persistence, you can create a ripple effect of positive change that transforms your life.

Practical Exercises

1. **Habit Audit:** Conduct a habit audit to identify your current habits. Make a list of your daily routines and categorize them as positive, negative or neutral. This exercise will help you become more aware of your habits and identify areas for improvement.
2. **Create a Habit Plan:** Choose one positive habit you want to cultivate and one negative habit you want to break. Create a plan for each habit, outlining the steps you will take, the triggers you will use and the rewards you will incorporate. Write down your plan and review it regularly to stay focused and motivated.
3. **Habit Tracker:** Use a habit tracker to monitor your progress. Create a simple chart or use an app to record your daily efforts. Tracking your progress visually can reinforce your commitment and provide a sense of accomplishment.
4. **Accountability Partner:** Find an accountability partner who shares similar goals. Schedule regular check-ins to discuss your progress, share tips and provide mutual support. Having someone to share your journey with creates a sense of responsibility and motivation.
5. **Reflection Journal:** Maintain a reflection journal to document your experiences, challenges and insights as you

work on cultivating good habits and breaking bad ones. Reflecting on your journey helps you stay mindful and make necessary adjustments. Writing about your progress and setbacks allows you to gain perspective and identify patterns that can inform your approach to habit formation.

By integrating these practical exercises into your daily life, you can create a supportive framework for building and sustaining good habits while breaking free from negative ones. Remember, the key to lasting change lies in the consistent application of small, intentional actions. Embrace the journey, celebrate your progress and trust in the power of habits to shape your life for the better.

3

The Journey of Habits: From Formation to Automation

Have you ever wondered why you instinctively reach for your toothbrush every morning or why your daily jog feels like second nature? It's all thanks to the brain's incredible ability to form and automate habits. Our brains are wired to create shortcuts for routine behaviours, allowing us to operate efficiently without expending too much mental energy. In this chapter, we'll explore how habits are formed, how they become automated, the importance of awareness in changing habits and how to ensure you don't forget anything. Plus, I'll introduce you to a nifty tool called the "habito-metre" to help track your progress.

The Brain's Role in Habit Formation

The brain is a remarkable organ, constantly adapting and reorganizing itself through a process known as neuroplasticity. This ability to change and form new neural connections is the foundation of habit formation. When we repeat an action over time, the brain creates stronger and more efficient pathways, making the behaviour easier to perform.

Example: Learning to Drive

Remember when you first learned to drive? Initially, it was overwhelming—checking mirrors, signaling, steering and maintaining speed all at once seemed like an impossible task. But with practice, your brain formed neural pathways that made these actions more automatic. Today, you probably drive without giving much thought to each individual task. This transformation is a testament to the brain's ability to form habits through repetition and practice.

The Piano Player

Take Sarah, for example. She started playing piano at the age of five. At first, she had to focus intently on reading the sheet music, placing her fingers correctly and keeping time. Her brain was working hard to create the necessary connections. Years of practice turned those complex tasks into second nature. Now, as an accomplished pianist, Sarah's fingers glide effortlessly across the keys, her brain having solidified the habit of playing.

The Phases of Habit Formation

To understand how habits are formed, let's break down the process into three distinct phases: the cue, the routine and the reward.

1. **Cue:** The cue is a trigger that initiates the habit. It can be anything from a specific time of day, an emotion, a location or an event. For instance, the sound of your alarm clock might be the cue to start your morning routine.
2. **Routine:** The routine is the behaviour you perform in response to the cue. This could be brushing your teeth,

going for a jog or checking your phone. The routine is the actual habit that you want to establish.
3. **Reward:** The reward is the positive outcome you experience after completing the routine. It reinforces the habit and makes it more likely to be repeated. For example, the feeling of cleanliness after brushing your teeth or the endorphin rush after a jog serves as the reward.

By consistently following this cycle, the brain starts to associate the cue with the routine and the reward, making the behaviour more automatic over time.

Example: Developing a Reading Habit

Let's say you want to develop a habit of reading every night before bed. Here's how you might apply the cue-routine-reward cycle:

- **Cue:** Setting an alarm for 9.00 p.m.
- **Routine:** Reading a book for 30 minutes.
- **Reward:** The satisfaction of completing a chapter and the relaxation that helps you sleep better.

By repeating this cycle consistently, your brain starts to associate 9.00 p.m. with reading, and eventually, the habit becomes automatic.

How Habits Become Automated

Once a habit is formed, the brain shifts the control of that behaviour from the prefrontal cortex (responsible for decision-making) to the basal ganglia (associated with habits and routines). This shift allows the brain to save energy and focus on more complex tasks.

Example: Morning Routine

Think about your morning routine. The sequence of waking up, brushing your teeth and getting dressed likely happens without much thought. These actions have become automated, freeing up mental bandwidth for other decisions you need to make throughout the day. This automation is the brain's way of making life more efficient.

The Marathon Runner

Consider John, a marathon runner. When he started running, each step required conscious effort. He had to focus on his breathing, stride and pace. After years of training, running became second nature. John's brain had automated the process, allowing him to run long distances without conscious effort. This automation not only improved his performance but also made running a more enjoyable experience.

The Importance of Awareness in Changing Habits

While the automation of habits is beneficial, it can also make breaking bad habits or forming new ones challenging. The first step in changing a habit is awareness. You need to recognize and understand your current habits before you can effectively alter them.

Example: Breaking a Bad Eating Habit

Let's say you want to break the habit of snacking on junk food while watching TV. The first step is to become aware of when and why you reach for those snacks. Are you genuinely hungry, or is it a response to boredom or stress? By identifying the trigger, you can take steps to change the behaviour.

The Mindful Shopper

Emma realized she had a habit of impulse buying whenever she felt stressed. By keeping a journal, she tracked her spending habits and identified the emotional triggers behind her purchases. With this awareness, Emma started practising mindfulness techniques, such as deep breathing and meditation, to manage her stress instead of resorting to shopping. Her conscious effort to be aware of her triggers helped her break the habit and save money.

Strategies for Increasing Awareness

1. **Journaling:** Keeping a habit journal can help you become more aware of your behaviours. Write down your habits, the cues that trigger them and the rewards you experience. This practice will give you insight into your routines and help identify patterns.
2. **Mindfulness:** Practising mindfulness can help you stay present and aware of your actions. Techniques such as meditation, deep breathing and body scanning can enhance your awareness of your habits and their triggers.
3. **Feedback:** Seek feedback from friends, family or colleagues. Sometimes, others can notice patterns and behaviours that you might overlook. Their observations can provide valuable insights into your habits.

Ensuring You Don't Forget Anything

In our fast-paced lives, it's easy to forget tasks or let important habits slip through the cracks. Here are some strategies to help ensure you stay on top of your habits and responsibilities.

Create a Routine

Establishing a routine can help anchor your habits and make them more consistent. By performing tasks at the same time each day, you create a rhythm that makes it easier to remember and maintain your habits.

Use Reminders

Set reminders on your phone or use sticky notes in visible places to prompt you to perform certain habits. For example, if you want to remember to drink more water, place a sticky note on your computer screen or set hourly reminders on your phone.

Keep a Journal

Writing things down can significantly improve your ability to remember tasks and track your progress. Use a journal to record your daily habits, tasks and goals. Reviewing your entries regularly helps reinforce your commitments and keeps you accountable.

The Organized Student

Mike, a college student, struggled with keeping track of his assignments and study schedule. He started using a planner to write down his daily tasks and deadlines. This simple habit of journaling helped him stay organized and on top of his responsibilities. As a result, his grades improved, and he felt less stressed about his workload.

Introducing the Habito-metre

To help you track your habits and ensure you're making progress, I've created a tool called the "habito-metre." This simple yet effective tool will help you visualize your habits and keep you accountable.

How to Use the Habito-metre

1. **List Your Habits:** Start by listing the habits you want to track. Include both good habits you want to cultivate and bad habits you want to break.
2. **Set Clear Goals:** For each habit, set a clear and achievable goal. For example, "Exercise for 30 minutes daily" or "Limit social media use to one hour per day."
3. **Track Daily Progress:** Create a chart with the days of the month along the top and your habits listed down the side. Each day, mark whether you successfully completed each habit. You can use checkmarks, stickers or even coloured dots to make it fun and engaging.
4. **Review and Reflect:** At the end of each week, review your habito-metre to see how well you did. Reflect on any patterns or obstacles that emerged and adjust your strategies accordingly.

Anecdote: The Productive Professional

Laura, a project manager, used the habito-metre to track her productivity habits. She listed habits such as "Review project plans daily" and "Schedule weekly team meetings." By visually tracking her habits, Laura stayed focused and consistent. Her productivity soared, and she felt more in control of her workday.

Strategies for Building Good Habits

Building good habits requires intention and consistency. Here are some practical strategies to help you cultivate positive habits that can transform your life.

1. **Start Small:** The key to building a new habit is to start small. Choose a habit that is easy to incorporate into your daily routine. For example, if you want to develop a habit of exercising, start with just five minutes of stretching each morning. As the habit becomes ingrained, you can gradually increase the duration and intensity.
2. **Be Consistent:** Consistency is crucial for habit formation. Commit to performing your chosen habit every day, even if it's just for a few minutes. The more consistent you are, the more likely the habit will stick. Use reminders, such as setting alarms or placing sticky notes in visible locations, to help you stay on track.
3. **Track Your Progress:** Keeping track of your progress can be highly motivating. Use a habit tracker or journal to record your daily efforts. Seeing your progress visually can reinforce your commitment and help you stay accountable.
4. **Find a Trigger:** Identify a specific trigger that prompts you to perform your habit. For example, if you want to develop a habit of flossing, use brushing your teeth as the trigger. By linking your new habit to an existing routine, you create a natural cue that reminds you to take action.
5. **Reward Yourself:** Incorporate immediate rewards to reinforce your new habit. Treat yourself to something enjoyable after completing your habit, such as enjoying a favourite snack or spending a few minutes on a hobby. Positive reinforcement can make the habit more enjoyable and increase your motivation to stick with it.

Strategies for Breaking Bad Habits

Breaking bad habits can be challenging, but it's possible with the right approach. Here are some strategies to help you overcome negative habits and replace them with positive ones.

1. **Identify Triggers:** The first step in breaking a bad habit is to identify the triggers that prompt the behaviour. Pay attention to the situations, emotions or people that lead you to engage in the habit. Once you identify the triggers, you can develop strategies to avoid or manage them.
2. **Replace the Habit:** Instead of simply trying to eliminate a bad habit, replace it with a positive one. For example, if you have a habit of snacking on junk food when you're stressed, replace it with a healthier alternative, such as going for a walk or practising deep breathing exercises.
3. **Change Your Environment:** Your environment plays a significant role in shaping your habits. Make changes to your surroundings to support your efforts to break a bad habit. For example, if you want to reduce screen time, remove electronic devices from your bedroom and create a designated space for screen-free activities.
4. **Seek Support:** Enlist the support of friends, family or a support group to help you break a bad habit. Share your goals and progress with them, and ask for their encouragement and accountability. Having a support system can provide motivation and make the process more manageable.
5. **Be Patient and Persistent:** Breaking a bad habit takes time and effort. Be patient with yourself and recognize that setbacks are a natural part of the process. Stay persistent and continue to focus on your goals, even if progress is slow. Celebrate small victories along the way to keep yourself motivated.

Conclusion

Our habits have a profound impact on our lives. Good habits propel us forward, helping us achieve our goals and improve our well-being, while bad habits hold us back and create obstacles to success. By understanding the power of habits and implementing practical strategies to cultivate positive habits and break negative ones, we can shape our lives for the better. Remember, the key to lasting change lies in the small, consistent actions we take every day. Start by identifying one good habit you can incorporate into your routine and one bad habit you want to break. With intention and persistence, you can create a ripple effect of positive change that transforms your life.

4

Building New Habits Upon Old Ones: The Power of Habit Stacking

We've all heard the saying, "Old habits die hard." But what if I told you that old habits could actually be your greatest ally in forming new ones? The secret lies in a concept called "habit stacking." By linking new habits to established ones, you can create powerful routines that are easier to maintain. In this chapter, we'll explore the art of habit stacking, providing practical strategies, real-life examples and historical anecdotes to inspire you on your journey.

What is Habit Stacking?

Benjamin Franklin, one of America's founding fathers, was known for his structured daily routine. He started each day with a question: "What good shall I do this day?" Franklin stacked this habit of setting daily intentions onto his morning routine of washing and dressing. This practice helped him stay focused on his goals and maintain a productive mindset throughout the day.

Habit stacking is a simple but powerful technique where you use an existing habit as a trigger for a new one. Instead of trying to build a new habit from scratch, you "stack" it onto a habit that is already ingrained in your routine. This makes the new habit more likely to stick because it's anchored to a behaviour you already perform consistently.

The Science Behind Habit Stacking

Our brains love routines. When we repeat a behaviour often enough, it becomes a habit stored in the basal ganglia, the part of the brain responsible for habit formation. This process allows us to perform routine tasks with minimal conscious effort, freeing up mental resources for more complex activities.

By attaching a new habit to an established one, you leverage the brain's natural inclination to follow patterns. This reduces the friction of starting a new habit and increases the likelihood of long-term success.

How to Build New Habits Upon Old Ones

1. **Identify Your Current Habits:** The first step in habit stacking is to identify the habits you already have. These should be behaviours that are well-ingrained and occur regularly without much thought. Examples include brushing your teeth, making your morning coffee or commuting to work.
2. **Choose a New Habit:** Next, decide on the new habit you want to form. It should be specific, manageable and ideally something that complements or enhances your existing habit. For instance, if you want to develop a gratitude practice, you might choose to write down three things you're grateful for each day.
3. **Create a Habit Stack:** Now, it's time to stack the new habit onto the old one. The formula for habit stacking is simple:

"After [existing habit], I will [new habit]." For example, "After I brush my teeth in the morning, I will write down three things I'm grateful for."
4. **Start Small and Be Consistent:** Begin with a small version of your new habit to make it less intimidating and easier to stick with. Consistency is key. As the new habit becomes more ingrained, you can gradually increase its duration or intensity.
5. **Track Your Progress:** Use a habit tracker to monitor your progress. Seeing your streaks build-up can be incredibly motivating and help reinforce your commitment to the new habit.

Real-Life Examples of Habit Stacking

Example 1: Enhancing a Morning Routine

Maria wanted to incorporate mindfulness into her daily routine. She already had a solid habit of drinking a cup of coffee every morning. She decided to stack a new habit onto this routine: "After I make my morning coffee, I will meditate for five minutes." By linking meditation to her coffee habit, she successfully integrated mindfulness into her morning routine.

Example 2: Building a Reading Habit

James, a busy executive, struggled to find time to read. He had a well-established habit of commuting to work by train. He decided to use this time to build a reading habit: "After I sit down on the train, I will read one chapter of a book." This simple stack helped him read several books over the course of a year.

Example 3: Increasing Physical Activity

Lisa wanted to become more active but found it hard to fit exercise into her busy schedule. She had a habit of watching

TV every evening. She decided to stack exercise onto this habit: "After I turn on the TV, I will do 10 minutes of stretching." Over time, she extended her workouts and enjoyed the benefits of regular physical activity.

Historical Anecdotes of Habit Stacking

Benjamin Franklin: The Virtue Chart

Benjamin Franklin, one of the Founding Fathers of the United States, was known for his commitment to self-improvement. He created a chart to track his progress in cultivating 13 virtues, such as temperance, industry and humility. Franklin used habit stacking to integrate these virtues into his daily life. For example, after his morning ablutions, he would review his virtue chart and plan his day accordingly. This routine helped him develop the habits that contributed to his success and legacy.

Stephen King: The Writing Routine

Prolific author Stephen King has a well-documented writing habit that has led to his incredible productivity. King writes every day without fail. His habit stack might look like this: "After I finish breakfast, I will sit down at my desk and write for three hours." By linking his writing habit to his morning routine, King ensures that he consistently produces new work, making him one of the most successful writers of our time.

Ludwig van Beethoven: The Coffee Ritual

Ludwig van Beethoven had a unique coffee ritual that he followed religiously. Every morning, he would count out exactly 60 coffee beans for his cup of coffee. This meticulous habit was part of his larger morning routine that prepared him for his composing work. By stacking this coffee ritual with his morning composition time, Beethoven created a consistent environment that fostered his creativity and productivity.

Practical Tips for Effective Habit Stacking

1. **Make It Logical:** Choose habits that naturally fit together. The more logical the connection, the easier it will be to remember and follow through. For example, stacking "After I take off my shoes, I will do 10 push-ups" makes sense because both actions are linked to physical activity.
2. **Use Visual Cues:** Visual cues can reinforce your habit stack. For instance, if you want to drink more water after brushing your teeth, place a glass of water next to your toothbrush. This visual reminder will prompt you to perform the new habit.
3. **Be Patient:** Building new habits takes time. Be patient with yourself and allow for gradual progress. If you miss a day, don't get discouraged. Simply get back on track the next day.
4. **Adjust as Needed:** If a habit stack isn't working, don't be afraid to tweak it. The goal is to find a routine that fits seamlessly into your life. Adjust the timing, location or sequence of your habits until you find a stack that works for you.

Overcoming Common Challenges

Challenge 1: Forgetting the New Habit

It's common to forget a new habit, especially in the beginning. To combat this, write down your habit stack and place it somewhere you'll see it regularly. You can also set reminders on your phone to prompt you at the right time.

Challenge 2: Lack of Motivation

If you find yourself lacking motivation, focus on the benefits of the new habit. Remind yourself why you wanted to incorporate it into your routine in the first place. Visualizing the positive outcomes can help reignite your motivation.

Challenge 3: Time Constraints

Time constraints can make it difficult to stick to new habits. Start with a small version of the habit that requires minimal time. As you become more comfortable, gradually increase the duration. Remember, consistency is more important than intensity in the beginning.

Personal Stories of Habit Stacking Success

Jane's Journey to Fitness

Jane, a mother of two, struggled to find time for exercise. She had a habit of waking up early to prepare breakfast for her family. She decided to stack a short workout onto her morning routine: "After I put the coffee on, I will do a 10-minute workout." By linking exercise to her existing habits, Jane successfully integrated fitness into her busy schedule. Over time, she increased her workout duration and saw significant improvements in her health and energy levels.

Mark's Meditation Practice

Mark wanted to develop a meditation practice to reduce stress. He already had a habit of enjoying a cup of tea in the evening. He stacked meditation onto this routine: "After I make my evening tea, I will meditate for five minutes." This small, consistent practice helped Mark manage stress and improve his overall well-being. As meditation became a regular part of his routine, he extended his practice and enjoyed even greater benefits.

Final Thoughts on Habit Stacking

Habit stacking is a powerful tool for building new habits upon old ones. By leveraging the routines you already have, you can create new behaviours with minimal effort. The key is to start small, be consistent and make adjustments as needed. With patience and persistence, you can transform your daily routines and achieve your goals.

Remember, the journey to self-improvement is a marathon, not a sprint. Celebrate your progress, no matter how small, and keep building upon your successes. With habit stacking, you're well on your way to creating a life filled with positive, lasting habits.

Practical Exercises

1. **Identify Your Habit Stacks:** Take some time to list your existing habits and the new habits you want to form. Write down potential habit stacks using the formula: "After [existing habit], I will [new habit]." Review your list and choose the stacks that make the most sense for your routine.
2. **Create a Habit Stack Chart:** Use a chart to visually track your habit stacks. List your habit stacks on the left side and the days of the week along the top. Each day, mark whether you completed the habit stack. This visual tool will help you stay accountable and see your progress.
3. **Reflect and Adjust:** At the end of each week, reflect on your habit stacks. What worked well? What challenges did

you face? Make adjustments to your habit stacks as needed to improve their effectiveness. Use this reflection time to celebrate your successes and plan for the week ahead.

Conclusion

Building new habits on top of old ones is a powerful strategy for personal growth and self-improvement. By leveraging the routines you already have, you can seamlessly integrate new behaviours into your life. Habit stacking simplifies the process of habit formation, increases consistency and reduces decision fatigue.

Remember, the key to successful habit stacking is to start small, be specific and celebrate your progress. Learn from historical examples and adapt strategies to suit your unique needs and lifestyle. With patience and persistence, you can transform your habits and achieve your goals.

Practical Exercises

1. **Identify Anchor Habits:** Make a list of habits you already perform consistently. These are your anchor habits that will serve as the foundation for new behaviours.
2. **Set Clear Goals:** Choose one or two new habits you want to build. Be specific about what you want to achieve and how you will measure success.
3. **Create Habit Stacks:** Pair your new habits with anchor habits. Write down the cue (anchor habit) and the new habit you want to perform immediately after. Use a habit tracker to monitor your progress.
4. **Reflect and Adjust:** At the end of each week, review your habit stacks. Reflect on what worked and what didn't. Make adjustments as needed to improve your approach.

5

How Our Environment Shapes Our Habits

Have you ever wondered why some habits stick effortlessly while others slip away despite our best intentions? The answer often lies not in our willpower, but in the environment around us. Our habits are profoundly influenced by our surroundings—social, political, cultural and even physical environments play a significant role in shaping our behaviours. In this chapter, we'll explore how various aspects of our environment affect our habits, delve into examples from professional life and share anecdotes that highlight the impact of social conditioning. We'll also discuss the importance of context in habit formation and offer practical strategies to harness environmental factors to our advantage.

The Power of Environment on Habit Formation

Our environment can either support or hinder our efforts to establish new habits. This includes the physical spaces we inhabit, the people we interact with, and the broader cultural and societal norms we live within. Let's break down how different aspects of our environment influence our habits.

Physical Environment

The physical environment includes the places where we spend our time—our homes, workplaces and communities. These spaces can be designed to promote or discourage certain behaviours.

Example: The Open-Plan Office

Open-plan offices have become popular in modern workplaces, touted for promoting collaboration and communication. However, they can also influence habits. For instance, the lack of private spaces might discourage focused, deep work, leading to habits of constant multitasking and distraction. Conversely, a well-designed office with quiet zones can promote habits of concentration and productivity.

The Fitness Buff

Consider Jane, a busy executive who struggled to maintain a consistent exercise routine. She decided to turn a corner of her living room into a mini-gym, complete with a yoga mat, dumbbells and a treadmill. By making exercise equipment visible and accessible, Jane's physical environment nudged her towards developing a daily workout habit. Over time, this small change in her environment led to significant improvements in her health and energy levels.

Example: The Clean Desk Policy

In many workplaces, a clean desk policy is enforced to promote organization and efficiency. By ensuring that employees start and end their day with a tidy workspace, businesses aim to cultivate habits of discipline and orderliness. This policy not only creates a more pleasant working environment but also enhances productivity and reduces stress.

Social Environment

Our social environment—the people we interact with regularly—has a powerful influence on our habits. We tend to adopt behaviours and attitudes that align with those of our social circle, often without even realizing it.

Example: The Corporate Culture

In a company with a culture that values long hours and constant availability, employees may develop habits of overworking and neglecting self-care. Conversely, a workplace that encourages work-life balance and wellness initiatives can foster healthy habits such as regular breaks, exercise and stress management.

The Smoking Room

In the 1960s and 70s, smoking was a common habit among professionals, often facilitated by designated smoking rooms in offices. As public health campaigns highlighted the dangers of smoking and workplaces began to ban indoor smoking, many individuals found it easier to quit. The shift in social norms and the physical environment played a crucial role in changing this deeply ingrained habit.

Example: The Gym Buddy System

In many fitness communities, the concept of a gym buddy system is encouraged. Having a workout partner increases accountability and motivation. When you know someone is counting on you to show up, you're less likely to skip your workout. This social support system helps individuals maintain their fitness habits and achieve their health goals.

Cultural Environment

Cultural norms and values shape our habits by defining what is considered acceptable or desirable behaviour. These norms can vary widely across different societies and communities.

Example: Eating Habits

In some cultures, communal meals and sharing food are central to social life, which can promote healthy eating habits and portion control. In contrast, cultures with a prevalence of fast food and eating on the go might foster habits of unhealthy eating and overconsumption.

The French Paradox

The "French Paradox" refers to the observation that despite a diet high in saturated fats, the French population has relatively low rates of heart disease. This paradox is often attributed to cultural habits such as savoring meals, eating smaller portions, and prioritizing fresh, high-quality ingredients. These cultural norms influence individual eating habits, contributing to overall health.

Example: Siesta Culture in Spain

In Spain, the tradition of taking a midday siesta is a deeply ingrained cultural habit. This practice allows for a rest period during the hottest part of the day, promoting better health and productivity. The siesta culture reflects the importance of balancing work and relaxation, a habit that contributes to the overall well-being of individuals in Spanish society.

Political Environment

The political environment, including laws, regulations and policies, can also shape our habits. Government actions can incentivize or discourage certain behaviours through legislation, taxation and public campaigns.

Example: Recycling Programs

Municipal recycling programs that provide convenient bins and regular pick-up services make it easier for residents to develop the habit of recycling. Conversely, areas without such programs may see lower rates of recycling due to the inconvenience and lack of infrastructure.

The Smoking Ban

In 2004, Ireland became the first country to implement a comprehensive smoking ban in workplaces, including bars and restaurants. This policy change significantly reduced smoking rates and influenced other countries to adopt similar measures. The political decision to create smoke-free environments helped many individuals break the habit of smoking by reducing social and environmental triggers.

Example: Plastic Bag Bans

Several countries and cities have implemented bans on single-use plastic bags to reduce environmental pollution. These policies encourage the habit of using reusable bags, which has led to a significant decrease in plastic waste. The political push towards sustainability helps shape individual behaviours towards more eco-friendly habits.

Social Conditioning and Its Impact on Habits

Social conditioning—the process by which individuals learn and adopt the behaviours, norms and values of their society—plays a crucial role in shaping our habits. This conditioning starts early in life and continues through various stages of development, influenced by family, education, media and peer interactions.

The Role of Family

Family is often the first source of social conditioning, shaping our early habits and attitudes. Parents and caregivers model behaviours that children are likely to imitate, whether it's brushing their teeth before bed, reading books or eating vegetables.

Example: Healthy Eating

If a family prioritizes healthy eating and regular physical activity, children are more likely to adopt these habits. On the other hand, families that rely heavily on fast food and sedentary activities may pass these habits on to their children.

The Generational Shift

In recent decades, there has been a noticeable shift towards healthier lifestyles. This change can be seen in families who now prioritize organic foods, regular exercise and mindfulness practices. Children growing up in such environments are likely to adopt these healthy habits as they mature, continuing the cycle of wellness into future generations.

The Role of Education

Schools and educational institutions play a significant role in social conditioning by instilling discipline, routines and values. Educational environments can promote positive habits such as punctuality, organization and a love of learning.

The Morning Assembly

In many schools, morning assemblies are a routine part of the day. This practice instills a habit of starting the day with a sense of community and focus. For students, the daily assembly becomes a cue for transitioning into a mindset ready for learning and engagement.

Example: School Gardens

Some schools have introduced gardening programs as part of their curriculum. These programs teach children about nutrition, responsibility and the environment. The habit of tending to a garden fosters a sense of accomplishment and a connection to nature, encouraging lifelong healthy eating habits.

The Role of Media

Media, including television, movies and social media influence our habits by shaping our perceptions of what is normal or desirable. Advertisements and content often promote certain lifestyles and behaviours.

Example: Fitness Influencers

Social media influencers who share their fitness routines and healthy lifestyles can inspire followers to adopt similar habits.

The visibility of these behaviours on social media platforms can normalize and promote the habit of regular exercise and healthy eating.

The Vegan Movement

The rise of veganism has been significantly influenced by media and social platforms. Documentaries like *What the Health* and *Forks Over Knives,* along with influential vegan bloggers and YouTubers, have sparked widespread interest in plant-based diets. The media's portrayal of veganism as a healthy and ethical choice has led many individuals to adopt the habit of vegan eating.

The Importance of Context in Habit Formation

Context is the backdrop against which our habits develop and thrive. The context includes the physical setting, social environment and cultural background that surround a behaviour. Understanding the context is essential for successful habit formation and change.

Contextual Cues

Contextual cues are the triggers in our environment that prompt specific behaviours. These cues can be objects, people, places or events that signal it's time to perform a habit.

Example: Desk and Work Habits

Having a tidy and organized desk can serve as a contextual cue for productivity and focus. In contrast, a cluttered and chaotic workspace might cue procrastination and distraction.

The Coffee Shop Writer

Many writers find inspiration and productivity in coffee shops. The ambient noise, the smell of coffee and the bustling environment serve as contextual cues for creative work. For these writers, the coffee shop becomes a space where the habit of writing is reinforced and made more enjoyable.

Context Change and Habit Disruption

Changing the context can disrupt old habits and facilitate the formation of new ones. This is why significant life changes, such as moving to a new city or starting a new job, often present opportunities to establish new routines.

The College Freshman

When Sarah started college, she saw it as a fresh start to adopt healthier habits. She used the change in environment to establish a routine of morning runs and regular study sessions. The new context helped her break away from old habits and build new, positive ones.

Example: The Digital Detox Retreat

Digital detox retreats are designed to help individuals break the habit of constant smartphone use. By changing the environment—taking participants to remote locations without internet access—these retreats provide a context where people can disconnect from technology and reconnect with themselves and nature. The new context makes it easier to develop habits of mindfulness, relaxation and face-to-face communication.

Strategies for Harnessing Environmental Factors

To effectively build and maintain habits, it's crucial to consider and optimize your environment. Here are some strategies to leverage environmental factors to your advantage:

1. Design Your Physical Space: Arrange your physical environment to support your desired habits. Make it easy to perform good habits and hard to engage in bad ones.

Example: Healthy Eating

Keep healthy snacks like fruits and nuts visible and easily accessible. Store junk food out of sight or avoid buying it altogether.

The Study Nook

When Emily decided to pursue a professional certification, she created a dedicated study nook in her home. She equipped it with a comfortable chair, good lighting and all the study materials she needed. By designing a space specifically for studying, Emily found it easier to develop a consistent study habit and stay focused on her goal.

2. Surround Yourself with Supportive People: Your social environment can significantly impact your habits. Surround yourself with people who support and encourage your positive behaviours.

Example: Exercise Buddies

Find a workout buddy who shares your fitness goals. Exercising with a friend can increase accountability and make the activity more enjoyable.

The Writing Group

Mark, an aspiring author, struggled with writing consistently. He joined a local writing group where members met weekly to share their work and offer feedback. The supportive community provided the encouragement and accountability Mark needed to develop a regular writing habit. Over time, this habit led to the completion of his first novel.

3. Leverage Social Norms: Use social norms to your advantage by aligning your habits with positive behaviours that are valued by your community or peer group.

Example: Professional Networking

If networking is valued in your industry, make it a habit to attend industry events and engage with peers regularly. The social norm of networking can reinforce your habit of professional engagement.

The Eco-Friendly Office

Linda worked in an office that prioritized sustainability. The company encouraged employees to reduce waste, recycle and use public transportation. The social norm of being eco-friendly influenced Linda to adopt these habits, both at work and in her personal life. The shared values of the workplace reinforced her commitment to sustainable living.

4. Use Technology Wisely: Technology can be a powerful tool for habit formation. Use apps and devices to set reminders, track progress and provide positive reinforcement.

Example: Habit-Tracking Apps

Use apps like Habitica or Streaks to monitor your habits and stay motivated. These apps provide visual cues and rewards that reinforce your behaviours.

The Pomodoro Technique

Alex, a software developer, struggled with procrastination and time management. He started using a Pomodoro timer app to break his work into focused intervals with short breaks in between. The app helped him develop the habit of working in concentrated bursts, improving his productivity and reducing burnout.

The Role of Political and Cultural Context

Understanding the broader political and cultural context is also important for habit formation. These factors can create opportunities or barriers to developing certain habits.

Political Policies

Political policies can facilitate or hinder habit formation by creating an environment that supports or discourages certain behaviours.

Example: Subsidized Gym Memberships

Some governments offer subsidies for gym memberships as part of public health initiatives. These policies make it easier for individuals to develop the habit of regular exercise by reducing financial barriers.

The Anti-Smoking Campaigns

Government anti-smoking campaigns have had a significant impact on reducing smoking rates. Policies such as higher taxes on cigarettes, graphic warning labels and public smoking bans have made it more difficult and less socially acceptable to smoke. These measures have helped many individuals break the habit of smoking.

Cultural Values

Cultural values and norms shape our perceptions of desirable behaviours. Aligning your habits with positive cultural values can enhance your motivation and sense of purpose.

Example: Mindfulness and Meditation

In cultures that value mindfulness and meditation, individuals may find it easier to adopt these practices. The cultural emphasis on mental well-being provides a supportive context for developing habits of mindfulness and meditation.

The Japanese Concept of Ikigai

The Japanese concept of ikigai, which means "reason for being," encourages individuals to find purpose and joy in their daily activities. This cultural value promotes habits of self-reflection, continuous improvement and pursuing passions. The widespread practice of ikigai in Japanese society supports habits that contribute to personal fulfilment and a sense of purpose.

Case Study: Building Professional Habits in a Supportive Environment

Let's explore a comprehensive case study to understand how the environment can shape professional habits.

Case Study: Sarah's Journey to Professional Growth

Sarah, a marketing manager at a mid-sized company, wanted to enhance her professional skills and advance in her career. She identified several habits that could help her achieve her goals: daily learning, networking and regular exercise to maintain her energy levels.

1. **Creating a Learning Environment:** Sarah transformed a corner of her office into a learning space. She placed industry-related books, a tablet for online courses and a comfortable chair in this area. By designing a dedicated learning environment, she made it easy to spend 30 minutes each day improving her skills.
2. **Leveraging Social Networks:** Sarah joined a professional association in her industry and attended monthly networking events. She also connected with peers on LinkedIn and participated in online forums. The social support from these networks reinforced her habit of continuous professional engagement.
3. **Incorporating Exercise into Her Routine:** Recognizing the importance of physical fitness for her overall well-being, Sarah joined a gym near her office. She scheduled lunchtime workouts and found a workout buddy among her colleagues. This social and physical environment supported her habit of regular exercise, which helped her stay energized and focused at work.

Over time, Sarah's efforts paid off. Her daily learning habits expanded her knowledge and skills, making her a valuable asset to her company. Networking opened up new opportunities and collaborations, while regular exercise improved her health and productivity. By optimizing her environment and leveraging social support, Sarah successfully built habits that propelled her professional growth.

Conclusion

Our habits are deeply intertwined with our environment. The physical spaces we inhabit, the social circles we move in, and the broader cultural and political contexts all play significant roles in shaping our behaviours. By understanding and harnessing these environmental factors, we can create supportive surroundings that make it easier to build and maintain positive habits.

Remember, the key to successful habit formation is to be mindful of your environment and make deliberate changes that support your goals. Design your physical space to encourage good habits, surround yourself with supportive people, leverage social norms and use technology wisely. Recognize the influence of political and cultural contexts and align your habits with positive values and policies.

By taking these steps, you can create an environment that not only supports your current habits but also fosters the development of new, beneficial behaviours. Embrace the power of your surroundings and let them guide you on your journey to a healthier, more productive and fulfilling life.

Practical Exercises

1. **Environmental Audit:** Conduct an audit of your physical, social and cultural environments. Identify factors that support or hinder your habits. Make a list of changes you can implement to create a more supportive environment.
2. **Design Your Space:** Choose one area of your life where you want to build a new habit. Design your physical space to support this habit. For example, create a dedicated workout area or set up a quiet reading nook in your home.
3. **Leverage Social Support:** Identify one or two people who can support your habit-building efforts. Share your goals with them and ask for their encouragement and accountability. Consider joining a group or community that shares similar goals.
4. **Use Habit-Tracking Tools:** Use a habit-tracking app or a simple journal to monitor your progress. Track your habits daily and celebrate small victories to stay motivated.
5. **Align with Cultural and Political Contexts:** Research policies and cultural practices that support your desired habits. Take advantage of any available resources, such as subsidies, programs or community initiatives, to help you maintain your habits.

By integrating these practical exercises into your routine, you can harness the power of your environment to build and sustain positive habits. Remember, the journey of habit formation is ongoing. Be patient, stay consistent and continuously adapt your environment to support your growth and well-being.

6

The Power of Self-Control: Mastering Habits for a Better Life

We've all heard the saying, "Old habits die hard," and it's true—changing ingrained behaviours can be challenging. At the heart of this struggle lies self-control, the ability to regulate our actions, emotions and desires. Whether you're trying to build good habits or break bad ones, self-control plays a crucial role. This chapter will explore the importance of self-control in habit formation, dive into the psychology behind it and share real-life examples and historical anecdotes to inspire your journey.

The Psychology of Self-Control and Habits

Self-control is the mental muscle that helps us stick to our goals and resist temptations. It's what keeps you from eating that second slice of cake when you're trying to lose weight or pushes you to hit the gym even when you'd rather stay in bed. But why is self-control so vital in forming and maintaining habits?

The Willpower Model

Psychologist Roy Baumeister's research on willpower and self-control reveals that self-control functions like a muscle—it can be strengthened with practice, but it also gets tired from overuse. This concept, known as "ego depletion," suggests that our self-control resources are finite. This is why, after a long day of making decisions, we might find it harder to resist unhealthy snacks or skip our evening workout.

Example: The Cookie Experiment

In a famous study, Baumeister and his colleagues placed two groups of participants in front of a plate of freshly baked cookies and a bowl of radishes. One group was allowed to eat the cookies, while the other had to resist and eat the radishes instead. Afterwards, both groups were asked to solve a difficult puzzle. The group that had resisted the cookies gave up on the puzzle much sooner than the group that indulged, demonstrating how exerting self-control in one area can deplete our willpower in another.

The Marshmallow Test

Another landmark study in the field of self-control is Walter Mischel's "Marshmallow Test." Preschool children were given a choice: they could eat one marshmallow immediately or wait 15 minutes and receive two marshmallows. Follow-up studies revealed that the children who were able to wait longer for the second marshmallow tended to have better life outcomes, including higher academic achievement and healthier lifestyles. This experiment highlights the long-term benefits of self-control and the ability to delay gratification.

Self-Control and Habit Formation

When it comes to forming habits, self-control helps us stay consistent until the behaviour becomes automatic. Initially, we rely on self-control to perform the new habit, but over time, it requires less conscious effort as it becomes part of our routine.

Example: Starting a Morning Routine

Imagine you want to start a habit of jogging every morning. In the beginning, it takes a lot of self-control to wake up early, put on your running shoes and head out the door. But as you repeat this behaviour, your brain starts to automate the process. Eventually, jogging becomes a regular part of your morning routine, requiring less mental effort to initiate.

Anecdote: Steve Jobs' Morning Routine

Steve Jobs, the co-founder of Apple, was known for his morning routine that included a series of small habits that set the tone for his day. He practiced mindfulness, had a healthy breakfast and planned his tasks meticulously. This routine required self-control initially but eventually became a source of stability and productivity in his life.

The Role of Self-Control in Quitting Bad Habits

Just as self-control is essential for building good habits, it's equally crucial for quitting bad ones. Bad habits often provide immediate gratification, making them harder to resist. Self-control helps us delay this gratification in favour of long-term benefits.

Example: Quitting Smoking

Consider the challenge of quitting smoking. The immediate relief from stress and the pleasurable sensation of nicotine make it difficult to resist. However, self-control allows individuals to endure the discomfort of withdrawal and the urge to smoke, focusing instead on the long-term health benefits. Over time, as the body adjusts and the cravings diminish, the need for self-control decreases.

Anecdote: The Story of Ulysses

One of the earliest examples of self-control comes from Greek mythology. Ulysses, aware of the irresistible allure of the Sirens' song, had himself tied to the mast of his ship and ordered his crew to plug their ears with beeswax. This story illustrates the concept of "Ulysses contracts," where we take preemptive actions to limit our future choices, thus exercising self-control by creating an environment that supports our long-term goals.

Strategies to Enhance Self-Control

While self-control can be depleted, it can also be strengthened through various strategies and practices. Here are some effective ways to boost your self-control:

1. Set Clear Goals: Having a clear, specific goal helps direct your self-control efforts. Vague goals like "exercise more" are less effective than specific ones like "run for 30 minutes every morning."

2. Create a Plan: A detailed plan outlines the steps needed to achieve your goal, making it easier to follow through. For example, if you aim to eat healthier, plan your meals and snacks in advance to avoid impulsive choices.

3. Monitor Your Progress: Tracking your progress helps maintain motivation and self-control. Use a journal, app or habit tracker to record your efforts and celebrate small victories along the way.

4. Practise Mindfulness: Mindfulness meditation can improve self-control by increasing awareness of your thoughts and impulses. This practice helps you pause before reacting, allowing you to make more deliberate choices.

Example: The Marshmallow Test

In the 1960s, psychologist Walter Mischel conducted the famous Marshmallow Test with preschool children. The kids were given a choice: eat one marshmallow immediately or wait 15 minutes and receive two marshmallows. The ability to wait, which required self-control, was linked to better life outcomes in follow-up studies. This experiment highlights the long-term benefits of practicing self-control and delaying gratification.

5. Avoid Temptations: Reduce the need for self-control by removing temptations from your environment. If you're trying to cut down on sugar, don't keep sweets in the house. The less you're exposed to temptations, the less likely you are to succumb to them.

Anecdote: The Story of Benjamin Franklin

Benjamin Franklin, one of America's Founding Fathers, is renowned for his disciplined approach to self-improvement. He developed a system of 13 virtues, focusing on one each week, and kept a journal to track his progress. Franklin's method of systematically working on his habits and avoiding temptations helped him cultivate a life of productivity and moral integrity.

Real-Life Examples of Self-Control and Habits

Let's look at some real-life examples where self-control played a pivotal role in forming good habits or breaking bad ones.

Example: The Athlete's Discipline

Elite athletes often demonstrate extraordinary self-control to reach the pinnacle of their sport. Take Michael Phelps, the most decorated Olympian of all time. Phelps maintained a rigorous training schedule, including swimming six hours a day, six days a week. His commitment to this demanding routine required immense self-control, but it enabled him to develop habits that led to unparalleled success in swimming.

Anecdote: Oprah Winfrey's Weight Loss Journey

Oprah Winfrey's battle with weight is well-documented. Her journey showcases the challenges of maintaining self-control over the long term. Through a combination of self-control, structured dieting and exercise, Oprah successfully lost weight multiple times. Her story highlights the ongoing nature of self-control and the need for persistence in the face of setbacks.

The Connection Between Self-Control and Emotional Regulation

Self-control is closely linked to emotional regulation—the ability to manage and respond to emotional experiences effectively. Our emotions can either support or undermine our self-control efforts, making it essential to understand this connection.

Example: Stress and Eating Habits

Many people turn to comfort food when stressed, seeking immediate emotional relief. This behaviour often leads to unhealthy eating habits. Developing self-control involves finding alternative ways to cope with stress, such as exercise, meditation or talking to a friend.

Anecdote: Mahatma Gandhi's Self-Discipline

Mahatma Gandhi is celebrated for his extraordinary self-control and discipline, particularly in the face of emotional and physical adversity. Gandhi practiced fasting as a means of protest and self-purification, demonstrating immense self-control over his bodily needs. His ability to regulate his emotions and remain steadfast in his principles inspired millions and played a crucial role in India's struggle for independence.

Building Self-Control: Practical Tips

Here are some practical tips to help you build self-control and enhance your habit formation:

1. Start Small: Begin with small, manageable goals to avoid overwhelming yourself. Successfully achieving small goals can build confidence and strengthen your self-control.

Example: Drinking More Water

If your goal is to drink more water, start by adding one extra glass per day. Once this becomes a habit, gradually increase your intake. This approach makes the goal more achievable and less daunting.

2. Use Positive Reinforcement: Reward yourself for maintaining self-control and achieving your goals. Positive reinforcement can motivate you to continue your efforts.

Example: Treat Yourself

If you stick to your workout routine for a month, treat yourself to something you enjoy, like a new book or a relaxing spa day. Rewards provide a sense of accomplishment and encourage continued adherence to your habits.

3. Visualize Success: Visualization can be a powerful tool for enhancing self-control. Imagine yourself successfully performing your new habit and enjoying the benefits. This mental rehearsal can increase your confidence and determination.

Anecdote: Arnold Schwarzenegger's Visualization

Arnold Schwarzenegger, the legendary bodybuilder and actor, used visualization to achieve his goals. He imagined himself winning bodybuilding competitions and succeeding in Hollywood, which motivated him to maintain his rigorous training and work ethic. Schwarzenegger's ability to visualize his success played a significant role in his achievements.

4. Seek Support: Don't be afraid to ask for help from friends, family or support groups. Having a support system can provide encouragement, accountability and practical advice.

Example: Weight Loss Groups

Joining a weight loss group, like Weight Watchers, provides a supportive environment where members share their struggles and successes. This communal support can enhance self-control by creating a network of accountability and motivation.

5. Practice Gratitude: Gratitude can enhance self-control by shifting your focus from what you lack to what you have. Regularly practicing gratitude can increase your overall well-being and help you stay committed to your goals.

Example: Gratitude Journal

Keep a gratitude journal and write down three things you're thankful for each day. This practice can improve your mood and reinforce your self-control by reminding you of the positive aspects of your life.

Overcoming Self-Control Challenges

Despite our best efforts, there will be times when our self-control falters. Understanding common challenges and how to overcome them can help you stay on track.

Challenge: Decision Fatigue

Making numerous decisions throughout the day can deplete your self-control, leading to poor choices later on. To combat decision fatigue, simplify your life by creating routines and minimizing unnecessary decisions.

Example: Simplify Your Wardrobe

Steve Jobs famously wore the same outfit daily—a black turtleneck, jeans and sneakers. By reducing the number of decisions he had to make, he conserved his mental energy for more important tasks. Consider adopting similar strategies, such as meal prepping or creating a daily schedule, to reduce decision fatigue.

Challenge: Stress and Emotions

Stress and strong emotions can undermine self-control, leading to impulsive behaviours. Developing healthy coping mechanisms can help you manage stress and maintain self-control.

Example: Deep Breathing Techniques

When you feel stressed or overwhelmed, practice deep breathing exercises to calm your mind and body. This simple technique can help you regain control and make more deliberate choices.

Challenge: Negative Self-Talk

Negative self-talk can erode your self-control and confidence. Counteract this by practicing positive self-talk and affirmations.

Example: Daily Affirmations

Start your day with positive affirmations, such as "I am capable of achieving my goals" or "I have the strength to make healthy choices." These statements can boost your self-esteem and reinforce your self-control.

The Long-Term Benefits of Self-Control

Developing self-control can lead to numerous long-term benefits, including improved health, stronger relationships and greater success in personal and professional endeavours.

Example: Financial Success

Individuals with high self-control are more likely to save money and make wise financial decisions. By resisting the urge to spend impulsively, they can build wealth and achieve financial stability.

Anecdote: Warren Buffett's Frugality

Warren Buffett, one of the world's richest men, is known for his frugal lifestyle. Despite his immense wealth, he lives in the same house he bought in 1958 and drives a modest car. Buffett's self-control and prudent financial habits have contributed significantly to his success.

Example: Academic Achievement

Students with strong self-control tend to perform better academically. They can resist distractions, focus on their studies and manage their time effectively, leading to higher grades and greater educational attainment.

Anecdote: J.K. Rowling's Perseverance

J.K. Rowling, the author of the Harry Potter series, demonstrated remarkable self-control and perseverance in her journey to becoming a published author. Despite facing numerous rejections and personal hardships, Rowling continued to write and refine her work. Her self-control and dedication ultimately led to her becoming one of the most successful authors of all time.

Conclusion

Self-control is a powerful tool in the formation of good habits and the elimination of bad ones. By understanding the psychology behind self-control, utilizing practical strategies and learning from real-life examples, you can strengthen your self-control and achieve your goals. Remember, self-control is like a muscle that can be developed and improved over time. With persistence and determination, you can harness the power of self-control to create lasting, positive changes in your life.

Practical Exercises

1. **Set Clear Goals:** Write down your goals and make them specific and measurable. Break them into smaller, achievable steps to maintain focus and motivation.
2. **Create a Plan:** Develop a detailed plan outlining the steps needed to achieve your goals. Include potential obstacles and strategies to overcome them.
3. **Track Your Progress:** Use a journal, app or habit tracker to monitor your progress. Record your successes and setbacks, and adjust your plan as needed.

4. **Practice Mindfulness:** Incorporate mindfulness meditation into your daily routine. Spend a few minutes each day focusing on your breath and observing your thoughts without judgment.
5. **Use Positive Reinforcement:** Reward yourself for maintaining self-control and achieving your goals. Choose rewards that are meaningful and motivating.
6. **Seek Support:** Share your goals with friends, family or a support group. Lean on them for encouragement, accountability and practical advice.
7. **Practice Gratitude:** Keep a gratitude journal and write down three things you're thankful for each day. Reflect on these positive aspects of your life to boost your mood and reinforce your self-control.

Integrating these practical exercises into your routine, you can strengthen your self-control and enhance your habit formation. Remember, the journey of self-control is ongoing. Be patient, stay consistent and celebrate your progress along the way.

7

Developing Irresistible Habits: The Science of Dopamine and Motivation

Imagine having a habit so compelling that you look forward to it every day with excitement and enthusiasm. Sounds impossible? It's not. The secret lies in understanding how our brains work, particularly the role of dopamine, and leveraging that knowledge to create habits that are not only beneficial but also irresistible. In this chapter, we'll explore the science of dopamine, how to incentivize yourself to form good habits, and share anecdotes, case studies and practical examples. By the end, you'll have a blueprint for developing habits you can't wait to dive into.

The Role of Dopamine in Habit Formation

Dopamine is a neurotransmitter often referred to as the "feel-good" chemical because it's associated with pleasure and reward. When you do something enjoyable, your brain releases dopamine, creating a feeling of euphoria. This process reinforces the behaviour, making you more likely to repeat it in the future.

Example: The Power of Anticipation

Dopamine isn't just released when you achieve a reward; it's also released in anticipation of the reward. Think about the excitement you feel when you're about to open a gift or start a vacation. This anticipation releases dopamine, which motivates you to pursue the reward.

Anecdote: Pavlov's Dogs

Ivan Pavlov's famous experiment with dogs demonstrated how anticipation can drive behaviour. Pavlov rang a bell before feeding his dogs, and eventually, the dogs began to salivate merely at the sound of the bell, anticipating the food. This response was driven by the release of dopamine in anticipation of the reward.

Making Habits Irresistible

To make a habit irresistible, you need to harness the power of dopamine by creating a strong association between the habit and a positive reward. Here's how you can do it:

1. Start with a Small, Enjoyable Activity: Choose a habit that is inherently enjoyable or pair a necessary habit with something pleasurable. The key is to start small and make sure the activity is something you look forward to.

Example: Reading with a Treat

If you want to develop a habit of reading more, start by pairing it with a small treat. Enjoy your favourite snack or a cup of tea while you read. The positive association with the treat will make the reading habit more appealing.

2. Set Clear, Achievable Goals: Having clear, achievable goals helps to create a sense of accomplishment, which releases dopamine. Break down your larger goals into smaller, manageable tasks that you can easily achieve.

Example: Running a Marathon

If your goal is to run a marathon, start with small, manageable milestones like running a mile without stopping. Celebrate each milestone to reinforce the behaviour and keep the dopamine flowing.

3. Use Immediate Rewards: The sooner you can reward yourself after completing a habit, the stronger the association will be. Immediate rewards help to cement the behaviour in your brain.

Example: Gaming and Exercise

Gamify your exercise routine by using apps that reward you with points or achievements. The immediate feedback from the app provides a dopamine boost that makes the exercise habit more enticing.

Case Studies of Irresistible Habits

Case Study 1: The Fitbit Phenomenon: Fitbit revolutionized how people approached physical fitness by turning exercise into a game. Users set daily step goals, received real-time feedback and earned badges for achievements. The immediate rewards and the anticipation of reaching new milestones created a dopamine-driven loop that made the habit of walking irresistible.

Case Study 2: Duolingo and Language Learning: Duolingo, a language-learning app, uses gamification to make learning a new language fun and addictive. The app provides immediate feedback, rewards streaks and offers badges for completing lessons. The anticipation of earning rewards and seeing progress keeps users engaged and motivated.

> *We are what we repeatedly do. Excellence,*
> *then, is not an act, but a habit.*
>
> —Will Durant

The Science of Incentives

Incentives play a crucial role in habit formation by providing the necessary motivation to initiate and sustain new behaviours. To effectively incentivize yourself, it's essential to understand the types of incentives and how to use them.

Intrinsic vs. Extrinsic Motivation

- **Intrinsic Motivation:** This comes from within and is driven by personal satisfaction and enjoyment. For example, reading a book because you love learning.
- **Extrinsic Motivation:** This involves external rewards such as money, praise or recognition. For example, exercising to lose weight or to earn a reward.

While both types of motivation can be effective, habits driven by intrinsic motivation are more likely to be sustained in the long term.

Example: Learning a Musical Instrument

Learning to play a musical instrument can be motivated intrinsically (enjoyment of music) or extrinsically (performing for others, earning accolades). Combining both motivations can make the habit more compelling and sustainable.

Strategies to Incentivize Good Habits

1. Find Your "Why": Understanding why you want to develop a habit provides intrinsic motivation. Reflect on the deeper reasons behind your goals and remind yourself of them regularly.

Example: Health and Fitness

If your goal is to get fit, think about the deeper benefits, such as improved health, increased energy and better quality of life. Keeping these reasons in mind can help sustain your motivation.

2. Create a Reward System: Set up a reward system that provides immediate, tangible rewards for completing your habit. Make sure the rewards are meaningful and motivating.

Example: Study Sessions

Reward yourself with a break, a favourite snack or some leisure time after a productive study session. The anticipation of the reward can make studying more enjoyable.

3. Use Social Accountability: Sharing your goals with friends or joining a community can provide external motivation and accountability. The support and encouragement from others can help reinforce your habits.

Example: Book Clubs

Joining a book club can make the habit of reading more enjoyable and consistent. The social aspect adds an extra layer of motivation and accountability.

4. Track Your Progress: Monitoring your progress helps you see how far you've come and keeps you motivated. Use journals, apps or habit trackers to record your achievements and celebrate your successes.

Example: Bullet Journaling

Bullet journaling is a popular method for tracking habits. By visually recording your progress, you create a sense of accomplishment that drives continued effort.

5. Gamify Your Habits: Turn your habits into a game by introducing elements of competition and reward. Gamification can make mundane tasks more engaging and fun.

Example: Habitica

Habitica is an app that turns habit formation into a role-playing game. By completing tasks, you earn points, level up and unlock rewards, making the process of building habits more enjoyable.

Anecdotes and Historical Examples

Anecdote: Jerry Seinfeld's Productivity Secret

Comedian Jerry Seinfeld developed a simple yet effective habit for writing jokes. He marked an X on a calendar for each day he wrote new material, aiming to keep the streak going without breaking the chain. The visual progress and the anticipation of continuing the streak provided a dopamine boost that made the habit irresistible.

Historical Example: Thomas Edison's Persistence

Thomas Edison, one of history's greatest inventors, had an incredible work ethic and habit of persistent experimentation. Despite thousands of failures, his relentless pursuit of innovation was driven by the small successes and the anticipation of eventual breakthroughs. Edison's ability to maintain such an enduring habit of experimentation was fueled by the dopamine-driven highs of each discovery.

Developing Your Irresistible Habit: A Step-by-Step Guide

1. **Identify the Habit:** Choose a habit you want to develop that aligns with your goals and interests. Ensure it's something you genuinely want to pursue.
2. **Set Clear Goals:** Define specific, achievable goals to give you direction and purpose. Break down larger goals into smaller milestones.
3. **Create Immediate Rewards:** Pair the habit with immediate rewards that provide a dopamine boost. Ensure the rewards are enjoyable and meaningful.
4. **Track and Celebrate Progress:** Use tools like journals, apps or calendars to track your progress. Celebrate small victories to keep your motivation high.
5. **Stay Flexible and Adapt:** Be prepared to adjust your approach if needed. Flexibility allows you to refine your strategies and maintain momentum.

Case Study: The Couch to 5K Programme

The Couch to 5K programme is designed to help non-runners gradually build-up to running a 5K. The programme's success lies in its structured approach and the use of incremental goals and rewards.

- **Clear Goals:** The programme is broken down into manageable increments, with each week building on the last.
- **Immediate Rewards:** Each completed run provides a sense of achievement and a dopamine boost.
- **Tracking Progress:** Participants use apps or journals to track their progress, reinforcing their commitment and celebrating milestones.
- **Support and Accountability:** Many participants join online communities or local groups, adding a social component that enhances motivation.

The journey of a thousand miles begins with one step.

—Lao Tzu

Takeaway

1. **Understand the Power of Dopamine:** Recognize how dopamine drives motivation and use it to make your habits enjoyable and rewarding.
2. **Start Small and Build Gradually:** Begin with small, achievable steps and gradually increase the complexity of your habits.
3. **Use Immediate Rewards:** Pair your habits with immediate rewards to reinforce positive behaviour and create a dopamine-driven loop.
4. **Leverage Social Support:** Share your goals with friends, join communities and use social accountability to stay motivated.
5. **Track and Celebrate:** Monitor your progress.

8

A Society of Habits: The Influence of Family, Friends and Celebrities on Habit Formation

Have you ever wondered why you suddenly picked up a new habit or why some behaviours feel so ingrained in your life? The answer often lies in the people around us—our family, friends, and even celebrities. These influences shape our habits, consciously and unconsciously, driving us to fit in and mirror those we admire. In this chapter, we'll explore the powerful role that family, friends and celebrities play in habit formation. We'll dive into the psychology of social influence, share real-life examples and provide anecdotes that illustrate these points. So, let's uncover how our social circles and society at large shape our behaviours.

The Role of Family in Habit Formation

Family is often the first and most influential social group we encounter. From childhood, our family members serve as primary role models, shaping our habits and behaviours.

Early Conditioning

Parents and siblings play a crucial role in early conditioning, instilling habits that can last a lifetime. The routines and norms established in the family environment become the foundation for our behaviours.

Example: Morning Routines

Consider the habit of a morning routine. If you grew up in a household where everyone woke up early, exercised and had breakfast together, you're likely to continue these habits into adulthood. This early conditioning creates a sense of normalcy around certain behaviours, making them easier to maintain.

Shared Activities

Family activities and traditions also influence habit formation. Whether it's a weekly family game night, regular walks or shared meals, these activities foster habits that emphasize family values and togetherness.

Anecdote: The Sunday Dinner

In many cultures, Sunday dinner is a cherished tradition. Growing up, Emma's family gathered every Sunday for a big meal, a habit that reinforced the importance of family time. As an adult, Emma continues this tradition with her own family, ensuring that the habit of gathering and sharing a meal remains a central part of her life.

The Impact of Friends on Habits

Friends significantly influence our habits, often through a process called social contagion, where behaviours and attitudes spread through social networks.

Peer Pressure and Social Norms

Peer pressure and the desire to fit in can strongly impact our habits. We tend to adopt behaviours that align with the norms of our friend group to gain acceptance and approval.

Example: Exercise Habits

Imagine you've joined a new friend group that prioritizes fitness. Seeing your friends regularly hitting the gym or going for runs can motivate you to adopt similar habits. The desire to fit in and be part of the group encourages you to embrace these healthy behaviours.

Shared Interests and Activities

Friends often bond over shared interests and activities, reinforcing certain habits. Whether it's a hobby, a sport or a lifestyle choice, engaging in these activities with friends makes them more enjoyable and sustainable.

Anecdote: The Running Club

Tom never considered himself a runner until his best friend invited him to join a local running club. Initially hesitant, Tom found that running with friends made the activity more enjoyable. The social aspect and the encouragement from his peers helped Tom develop a consistent running habit.

The Power of Celebrities and Social Media Influencers

In today's digital age, celebrities and social media influencers play a significant role in shaping our habits. We often look up to these public figures and imitate their behaviours, hoping to achieve similar success or status.

The Halo Effect

The halo effect is a cognitive bias where our overall impression of a person influences our feelings and thoughts about their character. When celebrities exhibit certain habits, we tend to view these behaviours positively and are more likely to adopt them.

Example: Health and Wellness Trends

Consider the influence of celebrities like Gwyneth Paltrow or Tom Brady, who advocate for specific health and wellness routines. Their endorsement of diets, fitness regimens or lifestyle products often leads fans to adopt these habits, believing that they will experience similar benefits.

Anecdote: The Yoga Craze

When Hollywood stars like Jennifer Aniston and Matthew McConaughey started practicing yoga, it sparked a widespread interest in the practice. Yoga studios popped up everywhere, and people flocked to classes, hoping to emulate the calm and fit lifestyle of their favourite celebrities. The habit of practising yoga, once considered niche, became mainstream, thanks in large part to celebrity endorsements.

Social Media and Influencer Culture

Social media platforms amplify the influence of celebrities and influencers, providing a constant stream of content that shapes our habits. We see curated glimpses of their lives, from morning routines to workout sessions, and often feel compelled to replicate these behaviours.

Example: The Rise of Veganism

Social media influencers like Ella Mills (Deliciously Ella) and Rich Roll have popularized veganism by sharing their plant-based lifestyles online. Their recipes, meal plans and personal stories inspire millions to adopt vegan habits, contributing to the growing popularity of plant-based diets.

The Phenomenon of Fitting In

The desire to fit in is a fundamental human instinct. We are social creatures, and being part of a group provides a sense of belonging and security. This need to fit in drives us to adopt habits that align with the expectations and norms of our social circles.

Social Identity Theory

Social identity theory, developed by Henri Tajfel and John Turner, suggests that individuals derive a sense of identity and self-esteem from their membership in social groups. We categorize ourselves and others into groups, adopt the norms and behaviours of these groups, and seek positive distinctiveness.

Example: Workplace Culture

In a corporate environment, fitting in with the workplace culture is crucial for social acceptance and career advancement. If the company culture values punctuality, teamwork and continuous learning, employees are likely to adopt these habits to align with their peers and succeed professionally.

Anecdote: The Tech Startup

At a tech startup, innovation and creativity are highly valued. Employees often work flexible hours, dress casually and collaborate in open office spaces. New hires quickly adapt to this culture, embracing habits that promote creativity and collaboration. Fitting in with the startup culture not only helps them integrate socially but also enhances their job performance.

Case Studies and Real-Life Examples

Case Study 1: The Influence of Family on Academic Habits

Sarah grew up in a family that placed a high value on education. Her parents were both educators, and study time was a well-established routine in their household. Every evening, the family gathered in the living room, each member working on their homework or reading. This environment instilled a strong work ethic and love for learning in Sarah, habits that she carried into her academic and professional life.

Case Study 2: Peer Influence on Healthy Eating

Jake, a college student, struggled with unhealthy eating habits until he moved in with new roommates who were health-conscious. Seeing his roommates cook nutritious meals and discuss health topics inspired Jake to change his eating habits.

He started meal prepping, eating more vegetables and reducing junk food. The positive peer influence helped Jake develop and maintain healthier eating habits.

Anecdote: The Celebrity Workout

When actor Chris Hemsworth shared his Thor workout routine, fans around the world took notice. Fitness enthusiasts and casual gym-goers alike began incorporating elements of Hemsworth's regimen into their workouts, hoping to achieve a physique similar to the Marvel superhero. The celebrity workout trend demonstrates how influential public figures can be in shaping our fitness habits.

The Social Dynamics of Habit Formation

Understanding the social dynamics that influence habit formation can help us create environments that support positive behaviours. Here are some strategies to leverage the power of family, friends and celebrities in developing good habits.

1. Create Supportive Family Routines: Establish family routines that promote healthy habits and positive behaviours. Whether it's a regular exercise schedule, family meals or study sessions, these routines can create a supportive environment for everyone involved.

Example: Family Fitness Challenges

Create a family fitness challenge where each member sets personal fitness goals and supports each other in achieving them. This can foster a sense of teamwork and accountability, making it easier to stick to exercise routines.

2. Surround Yourself with Positive Influences: Choose friends and social groups that support your goals and encourage positive habits. Being part of a community that values healthy behaviours can make it easier to adopt and maintain those habits.

Example: Joining a Book Club

If you want to develop a habit of reading more, join a book club. The social aspect and regular meetings provide motivation and accountability, making it more likely that you'll stick to your reading goals.

3. Leverage Celebrity Influence Wisely: Be mindful of the habits you adopt from celebrities and influencers. Ensure that these habits align with your values and goals, and seek out public figures who promote positive and realistic behaviours.

Example: Following Fitness Influencers

Follow fitness influencers who emphasize sustainable and healthy practices rather than quick fixes or extreme measures. Look for influencers who share valuable content, such as workout tips, healthy recipes and motivational advice.

The Importance of Context and Adaptation

While social influences play a significant role in habit formation, it's essential to consider your unique context and adapt habits to fit your lifestyle. What works for one person or group may not be suitable for another, so personalize your approach to habit formation.

Understanding Your Environment

Assess your environment and identify factors that support or hinder your habits. Make necessary changes to create a space that encourages positive behaviours.

Example: Home Office Setup

If you're trying to develop a habit of working from home more effectively, set up a dedicated workspace that minimizes distractions and promotes productivity. Ensure that your workspace is comfortable and equipped with the tools you need to succeed.

Adapting Habits to Fit Your Lifestyle

Customize habits to suit your preferences and lifestyle. Flexibility allows you to find routines that are enjoyable and sustainable in the long term.

Takeaways:

1. **Habits are Socially Contagious:** The people you surround yourself with—family, friends, and peers—can significantly influence your habits through imitation, shared values, and social norms.
2. **Celebrities Shape Aspirations and Habits:** Celebrities and influencers play a powerful role in shaping societal trends and personal habits.
3. **Community Support Enhances Habit Formation:** Supportive social environments, whether through family encouragement or peer accountability, create the emotional and practical foundation needed for habits to take root and flourish.

9

Find and Fix: Bad Habits and How to Overcome Them

We all have bad habits. Whether it's biting your nails, procrastinating or eating junk food, these habits can be frustrating and hard to break. But what if I told you that you could find the root cause of your bad habits and fix them for good? In this chapter, we'll dive into practical steps to uncover why you engage in these behaviours and how to address them effectively. We'll share real-life examples, motivational lines and anecdotes to inspire you along the way. Let's get started on the path to a healthier, happier you.

Understanding the Nature of Bad Habits

Before we can fix our bad habits, it's essential to understand why we have them in the first place. Bad habits often serve as coping mechanisms, providing temporary relief or distraction from stress, boredom or other negative emotions. These behaviours are usually triggered by specific cues and reinforced by immediate rewards, creating a cycle that can be challenging to break.

The first step to getting rid of bad habits is to understand that they are serving a purpose, even if it's a destructive one.

Example: Procrastination

Take procrastination, for instance. You might delay starting a project because the task seems overwhelming. The temporary relief you feel from avoiding the task is the reward that reinforces this habit. Understanding this cycle is the first step towards breaking it.

Identifying the Root Causes

To fix your bad habits, you need to identify their root causes. This involves examining the triggers, behaviours and rewards associated with the habit. Here's a step-by-step process to help you get started:

Step 1: Recognize the Trigger

The trigger is what sets off your bad habit. It could be a specific time of day, an emotional state or a particular situation. Pay attention to when and where your bad habit occurs to identify your triggers.

Anecdote: The Stress Eater

Consider Sarah, who realized she always reached for junk food when she was stressed. Her trigger was the stress she felt after a long day at work. By recognizing this, Sarah took the first step towards breaking her habit.

Step 2: Analyze the Behaviour

Next, focus on the behaviour itself. What exactly are you doing, and how does it make you feel? Write down your observations to get a clear picture of the habit.

Example: Nail Biting

If you bite your nails, you might notice that you do it when you're anxious or bored. The behaviour might provide a sense of relief or distraction, which is why you continue to do it.

Step 3: Identify the Reward

The reward is what you get from the behaviour. It's the reason you keep repeating the habit. Understanding the reward can help you find healthier alternatives that provide the same satisfaction.

> *Every habit, good or bad, is driven by a craving for a reward. Find the reward, and you can change the habit.*

Replacing Bad Habits with Good Ones

Once you've identified the root causes of your bad habits, it's time to replace them with healthier alternatives. This involves creating new routines that address the same triggers and provide similar rewards.

Step 1: Choose a Replacement Behaviour

Find a positive behaviour that can replace your bad habit. The replacement should be easy to implement and provide a similar reward.

Example: Stress Eating

Instead of reaching for junk food when stressed, Sarah decided to go for a walk or practice deep breathing exercises. These new behaviours helped her manage stress without resorting to unhealthy eating.

Step 2: Create a Plan

Develop a plan to implement your new habit. This might involve setting specific goals, scheduling your new behaviour and preparing for potential challenges.

Anecdote: The Proactive Planner

John wanted to stop procrastinating. He created a plan that included breaking tasks into smaller steps, setting deadlines and rewarding himself for completing each step. This proactive approach helped him stay on track and reduce procrastination.

Step 3: Track Your Progress

Monitoring your progress can help you stay motivated and identify any obstacles. Use a journal, app or habit tracker to record your efforts and celebrate your successes.

> *Small progress is still progress. Keep moving forward, one step at a time.*

Dealing with Setbacks

Changing habits is a journey, and setbacks are a natural part of the process. The key is to view these setbacks as opportunities to learn and grow, rather than as failures.

Example: Slipping Up

If you find yourself slipping back into an old habit, don't be too hard on yourself. Reflect on what triggered the setback and how you can address it moving forward.

Anecdote: The Persistent Quitter

Lisa struggled with quitting smoking. Despite several setbacks, she remained persistent, learning from each attempt and adjusting her strategies. Her determination paid off, and she eventually quit for good.

> *Success is not final, failure is not fatal:*
> *It is the courage to continue that counts.*
>
> —Winston Churchill

Strategies for Long-Term Success

To ensure lasting change, it's important to develop strategies that support your new habits and prevent relapse. Here are some tips to help you stay on track:

1. Build a Support System: Surround yourself with people who support your goals and encourage positive behaviours. Share your progress with friends or join a support group to stay accountable.

Example: Workout Buddy

Having a workout buddy can make exercising more enjoyable and provide the accountability you need to stick to your fitness goals.

Anecdote: The Accountability Partner

Mark wanted to write a book but struggled with consistency. He partnered with a friend who was also working on a project. They checked in with each other daily, offering support and encouragement. This accountability helped Mark stay motivated and finish his book.

2. Practice Mindfulness: Mindfulness can help you become more aware of your triggers and responses, allowing you to make conscious choices rather than falling back into old habits.

Example: Mindful Eating

If you tend to overeat, practicing mindful eating can help you become more aware of your hunger and fullness cues, reducing the likelihood of binge eating.

> *Mindfulness isn't difficult, we just need to remember to do it.*
>
> —Sharon Salzberg

3. Celebrate Your Successes: Recognize and celebrate your achievements, no matter how small. Celebrating your progress reinforces positive behaviour and boosts motivation.

Example: Reward Yourself

Set up a reward system for reaching milestones. Treat yourself to something special, like a new book or a day out, to celebrate your hard work.

4. Stay Flexible: Be open to adjusting your approach as needed. Life is unpredictable, and what works today might not work tomorrow. Stay flexible and adapt your strategies to fit your changing circumstances.

Example: Flexible Workouts

If your schedule changes, find alternative ways to fit in your workouts. Instead of a gym session, try a home workout or a quick walk during your lunch break.

Anecdote: The Adaptable Learner

Rachel wanted to learn a new language but struggled to find time. She switched from traditional classes to language apps that she could use on her commute. This flexibility allowed her to continue learning despite her busy schedule.

> *The measure of intelligence is the ability to change.*
>
> —Albert Einstein

Case Study: Overcoming a Bad Habit

Case Study: Jane's Journey to Overcome Nail Biting

Jane had been biting her nails for as long as she could remember. It was a habit she wanted to break, but she didn't know where to start. Here's how she approached the problem:

Step 1: Recognize the Trigger

Jane realized she bit her nails when she was anxious or bored. These emotions were her triggers.

Step 2: Analyze the Behaviour

She noticed that nail-biting provided temporary relief from her anxiety, which was why the habit persisted.

Step 3: Identify the Reward

The immediate reward was the sense of relief she felt. However, she also recognized the negative consequences, like sore fingers and embarrassment.

Step 4: Choose a Replacement Behaviour

Jane decided to use a stress ball whenever she felt the urge to bite her nails. The stress ball provided a similar sense of relief without the adverse side effects.

Step 5: Create a Plan

She kept the stress ball in her bag and at her desk, ensuring it was always within reach. She also set small goals, like going a day without biting her nails, and gradually increased the duration.

Step 6: Track Progress

Jane used a habit tracker app to monitor her progress and celebrate her milestones. Seeing her progress motivated her to keep going.

Step 7: Deal with Setbacks

There were times when Jane slipped back into her old habit, especially during high-stress periods. Instead of giving up, she reflected on what triggered the setback and adjusted her strategies.

Step 8: Build a Support System

Jane shared her goal with her friends and family, who supported her efforts and encouraged her along the way.

Step 9: Practice Mindfulness

She started practicing mindfulness to manage her anxiety better, reducing the urge to bite her nails.

Step 10: Celebrate Successes

Each time Jane reached a milestone, she celebrated with a small reward, reinforcing her progress.

Over time, Jane successfully broke her nail-biting habit and replaced it with healthier coping mechanisms.

Conclusion

Breaking bad habits and replacing them with good ones is a journey that requires patience, persistence and self-awareness. By understanding the triggers, behaviours and rewards associated with your bad habits, you can identify their root causes and develop effective strategies to address them. Remember to be kind to yourself and celebrate your progress along the way.

10

Repeat, Repeat, Repeat: The Power of Discipline in Habit Formation

Ever wondered why some people seem to effortlessly stick to their habits while others struggle to keep up? The secret lies in two key ingredients: discipline and consistency. These elements are crucial in forming lasting habits, whether you're trying to get fit, learn a new skill or develop a productive routine. In this chapter, we'll explore why discipline and consistency matter so much in habit formation, the importance of being slow but steady, the power of practice over planning and how repetition can transform your life. Let's dive in and uncover the secrets to building habits that stick.

Discipline: The Foundation of Habit Formation

Discipline is the ability to control your impulses, emotions and behaviours to achieve long-term goals. It's the driving force that keeps you on track even when motivation wanes. Without discipline, it's easy to fall back into old patterns and abandon new habits at the first sign of difficulty.

> *Discipline is the bridge between goals and accomplishment.*
>
> —Jim Rohn

The Importance of Discipline

Discipline helps you:

1. **Stay Committed:** It keeps you focused on your goals, ensuring you follow through with your plans.
2. **Overcome Obstacles:** It provides the strength to push through challenges and setbacks.
3. **Build Resilience:** It helps you develop mental toughness, making it easier to handle adversity.

Example: Early Morning Workouts

Consider Jane, who decided to start working out every morning. Initially, she was excited and motivated, but as the days went by, waking up early became challenging. Discipline is what kept Jane going. She reminded herself of her goals and the benefits of regular exercise, pushing herself to get out of bed and hit the gym, even on days she didn't feel like it.

Consistency: The Key to Lasting Change

Consistency is about performing the same actions regularly and reliably. While discipline gets you started, consistency ensures you keep going. It's the steady repetition of behaviours that ultimately leads to habit formation.

> *Consistency is more important than perfection.*
>
> —Mark Manson

The Importance of Consistency

Consistency helps you:

1. **Build Momentum:** Regular practice reinforces behaviours, making them easier to perform over time.

2. **Create Automaticity:** Repetition leads to habits becoming automatic, requiring less conscious effort.
3. **Achieve Long-Term Success:** Consistent actions lead to compounding results, bringing you closer to your goals.

Example: Learning a Musical Instrument

John wanted to learn to play the guitar. Instead of practising for hours sporadically, he committed to practicing for just 20 minutes every day. This consistent practice helped him improve steadily, and over time, playing the guitar became second nature.

The Power of Being Slow but Steady

In our fast-paced world, there's a tendency to seek quick fixes and immediate results. However, when it comes to habit formation, slow and steady wins the race. Taking small, manageable steps ensures sustainable progress and prevents burnout.

> *Slow and steady wins the race.*
>
> —Aesop

The Benefits of a Slow but Steady Approach

1. **Sustainable Progress:** Small steps are easier to maintain over time, leading to lasting change.
2. **Builds Confidence:** Achieving small milestones boosts your confidence and motivation.
3. **Prevents Burnout:** Gradual progress reduces the risk of burnout, keeping you energized and focused.

Example: Weight Loss Journey

Emily wanted to lose weight. Instead of going on a crash diet, she made small, sustainable changes to her eating habits and exercise routine. By focusing on gradual progress, Emily avoided the pitfalls of extreme diets and achieved her weight loss goals over time.

Practice Over Planning: Taking Action

While planning is essential, it's the practice that truly makes a difference. You can spend hours crafting the perfect plan, but without action, your goals will remain out of reach. Emphasizing practice over planning ensures that you're making tangible progress.

> *You don't have to be great to start,*
> *but you have to start to be great.*
>
> —Zig Ziglar

The Benefits of Emphasizing Practice

1. **Real-World Learning:** Practice allows you to learn from experience, making necessary adjustments along the way.
2. **Builds Skill:** Repeated practice helps you develop and refine your skills.
3. **Creates Momentum:** Taking action, even imperfectly, builds momentum and keeps you moving forward.

Example: Public Speaking

David wanted to become a confident public speaker. Instead of just reading books and watching videos, he started practising by speaking at small events and joining a public speaking club. Through consistent practice, he improved his skills and became a more confident speaker.

The Power of Repetitions

Repetition is at the heart of habit formation. The more you repeat a behaviour, the more ingrained it becomes. This process, known as habituation, is how habits transition from a conscious effort to automatic behaviours.

> *Repetition is the mother of skill.*
>
> —Tony Robbins

The Science of Repetition

Repetition strengthens neural pathways in the brain, making behaviours more automatic. This process involves:

1. **Initial Effort:** The first few repetitions require conscious effort and discipline.
2. **Formation Phase:** As you continue to repeat the behaviour, it becomes easier and more familiar.
3. **Automaticity:** Eventually, the behaviour becomes automatic, requiring minimal conscious effort.

Example: Driving a Car

When you first learned to drive, every action required conscious effort. Over time, through repetition, driving became second nature. Now, you can drive without thinking about every little detail.

Strategies for Building Discipline and Consistency

To harness the power of discipline and consistency, here are some practical strategies:

1. Set Clear Goals

Clear, specific goals give you direction and purpose. Break down larger goals into smaller, manageable steps to stay focused and motivated.

Example: Fitness Goals

Instead of setting a vague goal like "get fit," set specific goals like "run five kilometers three times a week" or "do strength training exercises every other day."

2. Create a Routine

Routines provide structure and make it easier to stay consistent. Establish a daily or weekly routine that incorporates your desired habits.

Example: Morning Routine

Create a morning routine that includes activities like exercise, meditation and reading. Having a set routine helps you start your day with positive habits.

3. Use Reminders and Triggers

Reminders and triggers help reinforce habits by prompting you to take action. Use alarms, notes or specific cues to remind you of your habits.

Example: Hydration Reminder

Set a reminder on your phone to drink water every hour. This simple trigger helps you stay hydrated throughout the day.

4. Track Your Progress

Tracking your progress helps you stay accountable and motivated.

Use a journal, app or habit tracker to record your efforts and celebrate your achievements.

Example: Habit Tracker

Use a habit tracker app to monitor your daily habits. Seeing your progress visually can boost your motivation and commitment.

5. Stay Flexible and Adapt

Life is unpredictable, and rigid plans can sometimes fail. Stay flexible and be willing to adapt your approach as needed.

Example: Adjusting Workouts

If you can't make it to the gym, have a backup plan like a home workout or a quick run. Adaptability ensures you stay consistent even when plans change.

Real-Life Examples and Anecdotes

Example: The Consistent Writer

J.K. Rowling, the author of the Harry Potter series, wrote consistently every day. Even when she was a struggling single mother, she maintained her writing habit. Her discipline and consistency paid off, leading to one of the most successful book series in history.

Anecdote: The Steady Painter

Claude Monet, the famous impressionist painter, exemplified the power of being slow but steady. He painted the same scenes repeatedly, capturing different lighting and seasons. This repetition and consistent practice helped him master his craft and leave a lasting legacy in the art world.

Example: The Disciplined Athlete

Serena Williams, one of the greatest tennis players of all time, attributes her success to discipline and consistency. She practices tirelessly, honing her skills through repetition and maintaining a rigorous training schedule. Her dedication has led to an illustrious career with numerous titles and accolades.

The Importance of Mindset

A positive mindset plays a crucial role in maintaining discipline and consistency. Believing in your ability to change and grow can help you stay committed to your goals.

> *Whether you think you can, or you think you can't—you're right.*
>
> —Henry Ford

Developing a Growth Mindset

A growth mindset encourages you to view challenges as opportunities for growth rather than obstacles. Embrace setbacks as learning experiences and keep pushing forward.

Example: Learning from Failure

Thomas Edison failed thousands of times before successfully inventing the light bulb. Instead of seeing these failures as defeats, he viewed them as valuable lessons that brought him closer to success.

The Role of Accountability

Having someone to hold you accountable can significantly boost your discipline and consistency. Share your goals with a friend, family member or coach who can provide support and encouragement.

Example: Accountability Partner

Find an accountability partner with similar goals. Check in with each other regularly to share progress, challenges and achievements. This mutual support helps both of you stay on track.

Anecdote: The Supportive Friends

When two friends, Rachel and Lisa, decided to train for a marathon, they became each other's accountability partners. They scheduled runs together, shared training tips and encouraged each other on tough days. Their consistent support and accountability helped them both complete the marathon successfully.

Celebrating Small Wins

Recognizing and celebrating small wins along the way boosts motivation and reinforces positive behaviour. Celebrate each milestone to keep your spirits high and your progress steady.

Examples of Celebrating Small Wins

1. **Fitness Milestones:** Celebrate when you reach new personal best in your workouts, such as lifting heavier weights or running longer distances.
2. **Learning Achievements:** Reward yourself when you complete a course or master a new skill.

3. **Daily Habits:** Acknowledge your efforts in maintaining daily habits, like drinking enough water or meditating regularly.

Conclusion

Discipline and consistency are the cornerstones of successful habit formation. By being slow but steady, emphasizing practice over planning and leveraging the power of repetition, you can build habits that last a lifetime. Remember to set clear goals, create routines, use reminders, track your progress, stay flexible and maintain a positive mindset. With these strategies, you'll be well on your way to developing habits that transform your life.

> *The secret of your future is hidden*
> *in your daily routine.*
>
> —Mike Murdock

Takeaway

1. **Embrace Discipline:** Use discipline to stay committed, overcome obstacles and build resilience.
2. **Prioritize Consistency:** Focus on performing actions regularly to build momentum and achieve lasting change.
3. **Be Slow but Steady:** Take small, manageable steps to ensure sustainable progress and prevent burnout.
4. **Practice Over Planning:** Emphasize taking action and learning from experience rather than overplanning.
5. **Harness the Power of Repetition:** Repeat behaviours to strengthen neural pathways and make habits automatic.

11

Stop That Procrastination: Forming Habits One Step at a Time

We've all been there. You have a task at hand, but instead of tackling it, you find yourself scrolling through social media, binge-watching your favourite show, or doing anything but what you're supposed to do. Procrastination is a common hurdle that can derail our efforts to form good habits. In this chapter, we'll explore how procrastination impacts habit formation, how to overcome it and how small habits can be developed one day, one moment at a time. Let's dive into the world of procrastination and habit formation with a relaxed and informal tone, making it easy and enjoyable to follow.

The Impact of Procrastination on Habit Formation

Procrastination is the act of delaying or postponing tasks, often leading to stress, missed opportunities and feelings of guilt. When it comes to forming new habits, procrastination can be a significant barrier. Here's how it impacts habit formation:

1. **Disrupts Routine:** Consistency is key to habit formation. Procrastination disrupts the routine necessary to establish new habits.

2. **Increases Stress:** Putting off tasks increases stress levels, making it harder to focus on forming new habits.
3. **Creates Negative Associations:** Procrastination can lead to negative feelings about the task, making it harder to engage in the habit regularly.

Anecdote: The Procrastinating Student

Think about Alex, a college student who constantly procrastinates on his assignments. He tells himself he'll start studying tomorrow, but tomorrow never comes. As deadlines approach, Alex becomes stressed and pulls all-nighters, leading to poor performance and burnout. This cycle makes it challenging for Alex to develop a consistent study routine, illustrating how procrastination hinders habit formation.

Understanding Why We Procrastinate

To tackle procrastination, it's essential to understand why we do it. Here are some common reasons:

1. **Fear of Failure:** Worrying about not doing a task well can lead to avoidance.
2. **Perfectionism:** The desire to do something perfectly can prevent us from starting at all.
3. **Lack of Motivation:** Without a clear sense of purpose or reward, it's easy to put off tasks.
4. **Overwhelm:** Large tasks can feel daunting, making it easier to procrastinate than to start.

Example: Fear of Failure

Sarah wants to start a blog but fears her writing won't be good enough. This fear leads her to procrastinate, and months go by without her making any progress. Understanding that her fear of failure is the root cause of her procrastination is the first step toward overcoming it.

Strategies to Overcome Procrastination

Overcoming procrastination involves changing your mindset and developing strategies to tackle tasks head-on. Here are some effective methods:

1. Break Tasks into Smaller Steps

Large tasks can be overwhelming. Break them down into smaller, manageable steps to make them less intimidating.

Example: Writing a Report

Instead of thinking about writing an entire report, focus on writing just one section. Start with an outline, then write them, and so on. Each small step completed builds momentum and reduces the urge to procrastinate.

2. Use the Pomodoro Technique

The Pomodoro Technique involves working for a set period (usually 25 minutes) followed by a short break. This method helps maintain focus and reduces the likelihood of procrastination.

Anecdote: The Busy Professional

John, a busy marketing professional, struggled with procrastination until he discovered the Pomodoro Technique. By working in 25-minute bursts with five-minute breaks, John found it easier to stay focused and complete his tasks efficiently. This technique helped him form a productive work habit, demonstrating its effectiveness.

3. Set Clear Goals and Deadlines

Having clear goals and deadlines provides direction and motivation. Make sure your goals are specific, measurable, achievable, relevant and time-bound (SMART).

Example: Fitness Goals

Instead of a vague goal like "get fit," set a specific goal such as "run three miles three times a week." Having a clear target helps you stay focused and motivated.

4. Create a Positive Environment

Your environment plays a crucial role in your ability to focus and stay productive. Create a workspace that minimizes distractions and promotes concentration.

Example: Decluttering

If your desk is cluttered, it's easy to get distracted. Spend a few minutes each day organizing your workspace to create a more conducive environment for productivity.

5. Reward Yourself

Rewards provide motivation and make tasks more enjoyable. After completing a task, reward yourself with something you enjoy.

Anecdote: The Motivated Student

Emily, a student, struggled with procrastination until she started rewarding herself after study sessions. After an hour of studying, she would treat herself to a favourite snack or a short walk. These small rewards kept her motivated and helped her develop a consistent study habit.

Forming Small Habits One Day, One Moment at a Time

Forming new habits doesn't require drastic changes. Small, consistent actions can lead to significant results over time. Here's how to develop small habits one day, one moment at a time:

1. Start Small

Begin with tiny habits that are easy to incorporate into your daily routine. The key is to make the habit so small that it feels almost effortless.

Example: Flossing One Tooth

If you want to develop a habit of flossing, start by flossing just one tooth each day. This small action takes minimal effort and is easy to build upon over time.

2. Use Habit Stacking

Habit stacking involves pairing a new habit with an existing one. This method leverages the power of your current routines to form new habits.

Example: Morning Coffee

If you want to start meditating, pair it with your morning coffee. After you brew your coffee, spend a few minutes meditating. Linking the new habit to an established routine makes it easier to remember and perform consistently.

3. Track Your Progress

Monitoring your progress helps you stay accountable and motivated. Use a habit tracker or journal to record your efforts and celebrate your achievements.

Anecdote: The Consistent Runner

Mark wanted to develop a running habit. He started by running for just five minutes each day and tracked his progress in a journal. Seeing his progress and celebrating each milestone kept him motivated. Over time, he increased his running time and developed a consistent exercise habit.

4. Focus on the Present Moment

Concentrate on performing the habit in the present moment rather than worrying about the future. This mindfulness approach reduces anxiety and makes it easier to stay consistent.

Example: Reading One Page

If you want to read more, start by reading just one page a day. Focus on enjoying the moment rather than stressing about finishing the entire book. This small habit can grow into a daily reading routine.

5. Be Patient and Persistent

Developing new habits takes time and effort. Be patient with yourself and stay persistent, even when progress seems slow. Remember that small, consistent actions lead to significant results over time.

Anecdote: The Patient Gardener

Linda wanted to start a garden but felt overwhelmed by the amount of work involved. She began by planting one flower each day. Over time, her garden flourished. Linda's patience and persistence paid off, illustrating how small, consistent actions can lead to big rewards.

The Importance of Mindset in Habit Formation

Your mindset plays a crucial role in forming and maintaining habits. A positive, growth-oriented mindset helps you stay motivated and resilient in the face of challenges.

1. Embrace a Growth Mindset

A growth mindset is the belief that your abilities and intelligence can be developed through dedication and hard work. Embrace this mindset to overcome obstacles and persist in your efforts to form new habits.

Example: Learning a New Language

If you're learning a new language, adopt a growth mindset by viewing mistakes as opportunities to learn and improve. This approach keeps you motivated and open to continuous improvement.

2. Practice Self-Compassion

Be kind to yourself when you encounter setbacks or make mistakes. Self-compassion helps you stay motivated and prevents feelings of discouragement.

Anecdote: The Compassionate Learner

Rachel, a novice baker, often felt discouraged by her baking failures. By practicing self-compassion and viewing each mistake as a learning opportunity, she stayed motivated and eventually became a skilled baker. Her journey highlights the importance of being kind to yourself during the habit-formation process.

3. Visualize Success

Visualization is a powerful tool for achieving your goals. Imagine yourself successfully performing the habit and enjoying the benefits. This mental rehearsal can increase your confidence and determination.

Example: Public Speaking

If you want to become a confident public speaker, visualize yourself delivering a successful speech and receiving positive feedback. This practice can boost your confidence and motivation.

Real-Life Examples of Overcoming Procrastination and Forming Habits

Example: The Proactive Student

Lisa, a high school student, struggled with procrastination and poor study habits. By breaking her study sessions into smaller tasks, using the Pomodoro Technique, and rewarding herself after completing each task, she gradually overcame procrastination. Lisa's consistent efforts led to improved grades and a stronger work ethic.

The Determined Writer

James, an aspiring writer, often procrastinated on his writing projects. He started by setting small, achievable goals, such as writing for 10 minutes each day. By tracking his progress and celebrating each milestone, James developed a consistent writing habit. Over time, he completed his first novel, showcasing the power of small, consistent actions.

Practical Tips for Maintaining Discipline and Consistency

To maintain discipline and consistency in forming new habits, consider these practical tips:

1. Set Clear Intentions

Clearly define your intentions and reasons for forming the habit. Knowing your "why" keeps you motivated and focused.

Example: Health Goals

If your goal is to eat healthier, remind yourself of the benefits, such as increased energy, better mood and improved overall health.

2. Create a Support System

Surround yourself with people who support your goals and encourage positive behaviours. Share your progress with friends or join a community with similar interests.

Example: Fitness Community

Join a fitness group or online community where members share their workouts, progress and challenges. This support system provides motivation and accountability.

3. Be Flexible and Adaptable

Life is unpredictable, and plans may change. Stay flexible and be willing to adapt your approach as needed.

Example: Alternative Workouts

If you can't make it to the gym, have a backup plan like a home workout or a quick outdoor run. Flexibility ensures you stay consistent even when circumstances change.

4. Celebrate Small Wins

Recognize and celebrate your achievements, no matter how small. Celebrating your progress reinforces positive behaviour and boosts motivation.

Example: Reward System

Set up a reward system for reaching milestones. Treat yourself to something special, like a favourite meal or a relaxing day off, to celebrate your hard work.

5. Reflect and Adjust

Regularly reflect on your progress and make necessary adjustments. This practice helps you stay on track and continuously improve.

The Reflective Learner

David, a software developer, wanted to improve his coding skills. He set aside time each week to reflect on his progress, identify areas for improvement and adjust his learning strategies. This reflective approach helped David stay focused and continuously improve his skills.

Conclusion

Procrastination can be a significant barrier to habit formation, but with the right strategies and mindset, it's possible to overcome it. By breaking tasks into smaller steps, using techniques like the Pomodoro Technique, setting clear goals, creating a positive environment and rewarding yourself, you can develop small habits one day, one moment at a time. Remember to embrace a growth mindset, practice self-compassion and visualize your success. With patience, persistence and consistent effort, you can break the chains of procrastination and form habits that lead to a happier, more productive life.

Takeaway

1. **Break Tasks into Smaller Steps:** Overcome procrastination by making large tasks more manageable.
2. **Use Techniques Like Pomodoro:** Maintain focus and reduce procrastination by working in short, focused bursts.
3. **Set Clear Goals and Rewards:** Define specific goals and reward yourself for achieving them.
4. **Embrace a Growth Mindset:** View challenges as opportunities for growth and stay motivated.
5. **Celebrate Small Wins:** Recognize and celebrate your progress to reinforce positive behaviour.

12

Say Hello to Good Habits and Bye-Bye to Bad Habits

We've all been there—trying to cultivate a good habit, only to find ourselves slipping back into old patterns. At the same time, those pesky bad habits seem to cling to us like gum on a shoe. But what if there was a way to make good habits inevitable and bad habits impossible? It might sound too good to be true, but with the right strategies, it's entirely achievable. In this chapter, we'll explore how to create an environment and mindset where good habits thrive and bad habits wither away. We'll draw on examples from famous personalities, sprinkle in some motivational quotes, and keep things informal and engaging. Let's dive in!

The Power of Environment

Your environment plays a crucial role in habit formation. The spaces we inhabit can either support our good habits or enable our bad ones. Imagine you're trying to eat healthier. If your kitchen is stocked with junk food, you're setting yourself up for failure. On the other hand, if you fill your pantry with nutritious options, you're more likely to make better choices.

Example: James Clear, author of *Atomic Habits,* shares the story of Brian Wansink, a food psychologist. Wansink's research found that people who kept fruit on their kitchen counter weighed less than those who kept junk food visible. By simply changing the environment, the likelihood of choosing healthier options increased dramatically.

> *You do not rise to the level of your goals;*
> *you fall to the level of your systems.*
>
> —James Clear

Actionable Tip: Take a look at your surroundings. Identify areas that trigger bad habits and make changes to support your good habits. Rearrange your space to make the good habits more convenient and the bad ones more difficult.

Make Good Habits Easy and Bad Habits Hard

One of the most effective ways to make good habits inevitable is to reduce friction. The easier a habit is to perform, the more likely you are to do it. Conversely, making bad habits harder to execute can help you break free from them.

Example: Stephen King, the prolific author, writes every single day. He made this habit easier by having a dedicated writing space and setting a consistent time for writing. By making writing an effortless part of his daily routine, he has penned countless bestsellers.

> *The secret to getting ahead is getting started.*
>
> —Mark Twain

Actionable Tip: Think about a good habit you want to develop. How can you make it easier? Can you prepare the night before?

Set up reminders? Similarly, for a bad habit, consider how you can add obstacles. If you want to reduce screen time, put your phone in another room.

Leverage the Power of Routine

Routine is the backbone of habit formation. When a behaviour becomes a regular part of your schedule, it turns into a habit. Establishing a routine helps you automate good habits and minimize the effort required to maintain them.

Example: Tim Ferriss, author of *The 4-Hour Workweek* is a big advocate for morning routines. He believes that having a consistent morning routine sets the tone for a productive day. Ferriss' routine includes activities like meditation, exercise and journaling, which help him start the day on a positive note.

> *The chains of habit are too weak to be felt until they are too strong to be broken.*
>
> —Samuel Johnson

Actionable Tip: Design a daily routine that incorporates your desired habits. Start small and gradually build-up. Consistency is key. Once a habit becomes a regular part of your routine, it will feel effortless.

Use Positive Reinforcement

Positive reinforcement is a powerful tool for habit formation. Rewarding yourself for completing a good habit can reinforce the behaviour and make it more likely to stick. The key is to choose rewards that are meaningful and motivating for you.

Example: Charles Duhigg, in his book *The Power of Habit* talks about how he used the reward system to create a running habit. After each run, he allowed himself to enjoy a small piece of chocolate. This reward made the habit of running more appealing and helped him stick to it.

Actionable Tip: Identify a reward that you can associate with your good habit. It doesn't have to be extravagant—sometimes, a simple acknowledgment of your effort is enough. Make sure the reward is something you genuinely look forward to.

Accountability and Social Support

Having someone to hold you accountable can significantly boost your chances of forming good habits. Social support provides encouragement, motivation and a sense of responsibility. Whether it's a friend, family member or a community, sharing your goals with others can make a big difference.

Example: Arnold Schwarzenegger often credits his success to his training partners. Having someone to work out with kept him accountable and pushed him to achieve more. The camaraderie and competition among his peers were instrumental in his bodybuilding success.

> *Surround yourself with only people who*
> *are going to lift you higher.*
>
> —Oprah Winfrey

Actionable Tip: Share your habit goals with a friend or join a group of like-minded individuals. Regular check-ins can help you stay on track and provide the support you need to keep going.

Automate and Use Technology

In today's digital age, technology can be a great ally in habit formation. There are numerous apps and tools designed to help you track, remind and reinforce good habits. Automation can take the effort out of remembering and executing your habits.

Example: Jerry Seinfeld uses a simple method called "Don't Break the Chain" to stay consistent with his writing. He marks an 'X' on a calendar for every day he writes. The visual chain of 'X's motivates him to keep going. Nowadays, there are apps like Habitica and HabitBull that can help you create similar tracking systems.

> *Success is the sum of small efforts,*
> *repeated day in and day out.*
>
> —Robert Collier

Actionable Tip: Explore habit-tracking apps that suit your needs. Set reminders and use automated systems to help you stick to your habits. The less you have to think about it, the more likely you'll follow through.

Replace Bad Habits with Good Ones

Instead of trying to eliminate a bad habit outright, replace it with a good one. This technique is effective because it addresses the underlying need or craving that the bad habit fulfils while providing a healthier alternative.

Example: Shaquille O'Neal, the basketball legend, struggled with unhealthy eating habits. He decided to replace his late-night snacking with healthier options like fruits and nuts. By satisfying his cravings with nutritious alternatives, he managed to improve his diet without feeling deprived.

> *Bad habits are like a comfortable bed,*
> *easy to get into, but hard to get out of.*
>
> —Anonymous

Actionable Tip: Identify the trigger and reward associated with your bad habit. Find a good habit that can replace it and provide a similar reward. Gradually transition from the bad habit to the good one, ensuring the underlying need is still met.

Mindfulness and Self-Awareness

Being mindful and aware of your habits is essential for making lasting changes. Self-awareness allows you to recognize patterns and triggers, giving you the power to intervene and make conscious choices.

Example: Oprah Winfrey practices mindfulness to stay aware of her habits. She uses meditation and journaling to reflect on her actions and intentions. This practice helps her stay grounded and make deliberate choices that align with her goals.

> *The first step toward change is awareness.*
> *The second step is acceptance.*
>
> —Nathaniel Branden

Actionable Tip: Incorporate mindfulness practices into your daily routine. Take time to reflect on your habits and identify areas for improvement. Being present and aware can help you make intentional changes rather than acting on autopilot.

Patience and Persistence

Building good habits and breaking bad ones is a journey that requires patience and persistence. It's important to remember that change doesn't happen overnight. There will be setbacks, but staying committed and resilient is key to long-term success.

Example: J.K. Rowling faced numerous rejections before *Harry Potter* was published. Despite the setbacks, she persisted and kept writing. Her perseverance paid off, and she became one of the most successful authors of all time.

> *It's not that I'm so smart, it's just that*
> *I stay with problems longer.*
>
> —Albert Einstein

Actionable Tip: Be patient with yourself. Understand that setbacks are part of the process. Keep pushing forward, and don't give up. Celebrate small victories along the way to stay motivated.

Conclusion: The Five-Point Takeaway

1. **Optimize Your Environment:** Make good habits easier and bad habits harder by changing your surroundings.
2. **Routine and Consistency:** Establish a routine to automate good habits and minimize effort.
3. **Positive Reinforcement:** Reward yourself for completing good habits to reinforce the behaviour.
4. **Accountability:** Seek social support and share your goals with others to stay motivated.
5. **Mindfulness and Persistence:** Stay aware of your habits, be patient and persist through setbacks.

13

How to Make Any Habits Rewarding and Satisfying

Creating good habits can sometimes feel like an uphill battle. We know what we should be doing, but the lure of instant gratification often pulls us in the opposite direction. The secret to making good habits stick is to make them rewarding and satisfying. By incentivizing ourselves effectively, we can turn those uphill battles into enjoyable journeys. In this chapter, we'll explore various techniques to make any habit rewarding, drawing on real-life examples, anecdotes from famous people and practical tips. Let's dive in and discover how to make good habits a joy rather than a chore.

The Psychology of Rewards

Understanding why rewards work is the first step in making habits rewarding. Our brains are wired to seek pleasure and avoid pain. When we receive a reward, our brains release dopamine, the feel-good chemical that reinforces the behaviour and makes us want to repeat it.

Example: Think about the last time you received praise at work. That warm, fuzzy feeling you got wasn't just your imagination; it was your brain releasing dopamine. This reinforcement makes you more likely to repeat the behaviour that earned you the praise.

Actionable Tip: Identify small rewards that make you feel good and use them to reinforce your good habits. It could be something as simple as a piece of chocolate, a short break or even just a moment of acknowledgment.

Immediate Rewards for Long-Term Goals

One of the biggest challenges in forming good habits is that the benefits are often long-term, while the effort is immediate. To bridge this gap, it's crucial to find ways to provide immediate rewards for actions that contribute to long-term goals.

Example: Let's say you're trying to get in shape. The long-term reward is better health and fitness, but that can take months to achieve. To stay motivated, you might reward yourself with a relaxing bath or a favourite healthy snack after each workout session.

Actionable Tip: Break down your long-term goals into smaller, manageable tasks. After completing each task, give yourself a small reward. This immediate gratification will keep you motivated and moving towards your ultimate goal.

The Power of Positive Reinforcement

Positive reinforcement is a powerful tool for habit formation. By associating a habit with positive outcomes, you can train your brain to enjoy the process.

Example: B.F. Skinner, a renowned psychologist, demonstrated the power of positive reinforcement through his work with animals. He found that behaviours followed by positive reinforcement were more likely to be repeated. This principle applies to humans too.

Anecdote: My friend Sarah used positive reinforcement to build a reading habit. She loves coffee, so she decided to only allow herself a cup of her favourite brew when she sat down to read. Soon, her brain started associating reading with the pleasure of drinking coffee, making it easier to stick to her reading habit.

> *People often say that motivation doesn't last. Well, neither does bathing—that's why we recommend it daily.*
>
> —Zig Ziglar

Actionable Tip: Identify something you enjoy and pair it with the habit you're trying to build. This could be listening to your favourite music while exercising, watching an episode of a TV show after completing a work task or treating yourself to a small dessert after eating a healthy meal.

Social Rewards and Accountability

Humans are social creatures, and we thrive on social interaction and approval. Social rewards, such as praise and recognition from others, can be incredibly motivating.

Example: Think about social media. Every time you get a like or a comment, it feels good, doesn't it? That's because social validation triggers the release of dopamine. You can leverage this principle to build good habits by involving others in your journey.

Anecdote: When I decided to start running, I joined a local running group. Every time I completed a run, I'd post about it in the group. The likes, comments, and encouragement from other members made running feel rewarding and kept me motivated.

Actionable Tip: Share your goals with friends, family, or a community. Celebrate your successes together and seek encouragement when you need it. Knowing that others are cheering you on can make a big difference.

Gamify Your Habits

Gamification is the process of turning tasks into a game to make them more engaging and enjoyable. By adding elements of competition and rewards, you can make even the most mundane habits exciting.

Example: Many fitness apps use gamification to keep users engaged. They offer points, badges and leaderboards to turn workouts into a fun competition. This approach not only makes exercise more enjoyable but also provides a sense of accomplishment.

Anecdote: My cousin Mark struggled with staying organized until he discovered a task management app that gamified productivity. The app awarded points for completing tasks and allowed him to level up. Mark found himself eagerly completing tasks just to earn points and unlock new levels.

> *Motivation is what gets you started.*
> *Habit is what keeps you going.*
>
> —Jim Ryun

Actionable Tip: Find ways to gamify your habits. Use apps that turn tasks into games or create your own reward system with points and levels. Competing with yourself or others can add a fun and motivating twist to habit formation.

Visualize Your Progress

Visualizing your progress can be a powerful motivator. Seeing how far you've come can provide a sense of achievement and encourage you to keep going.

Example: Jerry Seinfeld uses a simple but effective method called "Don't Break the Chain." He marks an 'X' on a calendar for every day he writes. The visual chain of 'X's motivates him to keep writing daily.

Anecdote: My friend Emily uses a habit tracker app that shows her progress over time. Seeing the streaks of successful days gives her a sense of accomplishment and motivates her to maintain her habits.

> *It's not what we do once in a while that shapes our lives. It's what we do consistently.*
>
> —Tony Robbins

Actionable Tip: Use a habit tracker, calendar or journal to visualize your progress. Mark off each day you complete your habit and watch the chain grow. The visual representation of your efforts can be incredibly satisfying.

Reward Yourself with Breaks

Sometimes, the best reward is simply taking a break. Giving yourself permission to rest can be a powerful incentive to stay consistent with your habits.

Example: The Pomodoro Technique is a time management method that uses breaks as rewards. You work for 25 minutes and then take a five-minute break. After four cycles, you take a longer break. This approach makes work more manageable and rewarding.

Anecdote: When I was writing my first book, I used the Pomodoro Technique. The promise of a break kept me focused and productive. I'd reward myself with a short walk, a quick chat with a friend or a few minutes of relaxation.

> *Take rest; a field that has rested gives a bountiful crop.*
>
> —Ovid

Actionable Tip: Implement the Pomodoro Technique or a similar method that includes breaks. Use breaks as a reward for completing focused work sessions. This can help you stay productive and prevent burnout.

Financial Incentives

Money can be a powerful motivator. While it's not always practical, finding ways to incorporate financial incentives can add a tangible reward to your habits.

Example: Some people use apps that pay them to exercise or save money. For instance, apps like Sweatcoin reward users with virtual currency for physical activity, which can be redeemed for goods or services.

Anecdote: My friend Jake wanted to save more money, so he set up an automatic transfer to his savings account every time he resisted the urge to buy coffee. Seeing his savings grow was a satisfying reward that motivated him to keep up the habit.

> *The habit of saving is itself an education; it fosters every virtue, teaches self-denial, cultivates the sense of order, trains to forethought, and so broadens the mind.*
>
> —T.T. Munger

Actionable Tip: Find ways to incorporate financial rewards into your habits. This could be setting aside money for a treat each time you complete a habit or using apps that offer financial incentives. The tangible reward can be highly motivating.

Creating a Rewarding Ritual

Turning your habits into rituals can make them more enjoyable and satisfying. Rituals add a sense of ceremony and significance to your actions, making them feel special.

Example: Marie Kondo, the organization guru, has a ritual for tidying up. She treats each item with respect, thanking it for its service before deciding whether to keep or discard it. This ritual makes the act of tidying up more meaningful and rewarding.

Anecdote: My aunt has a morning ritual that includes brewing a cup of her favourite tea, reading a few pages of a book and doing some light stretching. This ritual not only helps her wake up but also makes her mornings feel luxurious and enjoyable.

> *A daily ritual is a way of saying, I'm voting for myself; I'm taking care of myself.*
>
> —Mariel Hemingway

Actionable Tip: Create a ritual around your habits. It could be a morning routine, a bedtime ritual or a special way to start your workday. Adding a sense of ceremony can make your habits feel more rewarding and satisfying.

Embrace the Power of Small Wins

Celebrating small wins can provide a constant stream of motivation. Recognizing and rewarding even the smallest achievements keeps you engaged and positive.

Example: Basketball coach Pat Riley used the concept of "incremental improvement" to lead the Los Angeles Lakers to victory. By focusing on small, consistent improvements, he built a winning team.

Anecdote: My colleague Lisa set a goal to write a novel. Instead of focusing on the daunting task of writing an entire book, she celebrated each completed chapter with a small reward, like a dinner out or a new book. These small wins kept her motivated and excited about her progress.

> *Little by little, one travels far.*
>
> —J.R.R. Tolkien

Actionable Tip: Break your goals into small, achievable milestones. Celebrate each milestone with a reward, no matter how small. This will keep you motivated and make the journey to your larger goal more enjoyable.

Incorporate Novelty and Variety

Routine can sometimes lead to boredom, which can make it hard to stick to habits. Incorporating novelty and variety can keep things interesting and rewarding.

Example: Fitness enthusiasts often switch up their workouts to avoid plateaus and keep things exciting. Trying new exercises, sports or classes can make staying fit more enjoyable.

Anecdote: My friend Tom wanted to read more, but he found himself getting bored with the same genres. He started exploring different types of books, from science fiction to biographies, and even graphic novels. This variety kept his reading habit fresh and exciting.

> *Variety's the very spice of life, that gives it all its flavor.*
>
> —William Cowper

Actionable Tip: Add variety to your habits. If you're exercising, try new workouts. If you're reading, explore different genres. Mixing things up can make your habits feel new and rewarding.

Conclusion

To make habits rewarding and satisfying, start by understanding the psychology of rewards and how they reinforce behavior. Break down long-term goals into smaller tasks and provide immediate rewards to stay motivated. Share your progress with others to leverage social rewards and accountability, and celebrate your successes together. Gamify your habits by turning tasks into engaging and enjoyable activities. Recognize small wins and incorporate variety to keep things fresh and exciting. By finding joy in the journey and celebrating each step, you can transform habits into enjoyable parts of your daily routine, ensuring lasting and meaningful change.

14

How to Keep Your Habits on Track and Bounce Back Quickly

Sticking to new habits can be challenging. Even with the best intentions, life has a way of throwing curveballs that can derail our progress. The key to long-term success in habit formation is not only establishing and maintaining good habits but also knowing how to get back on track when we slip. This chapter will delve into strategies to ensure that your habits stay on track and provide practical advice on bouncing back quickly after a setback. We'll explore real-life examples, share anecdotes and offer actionable tips to help you stay consistent and resilient.

The Importance of Tracking Habits

Tracking your habits is a fundamental strategy for ensuring they stay on course. When you keep a record of your habits, you create a visual reminder of your progress and a sense of accountability.

Example: Benjamin Franklin, one of the Founding Fathers of the United States, was known for his habit-tracking method. He kept a daily journal where he tracked 13 virtues he wanted to cultivate. This practice helped him stay focused and accountable.

What gets measured gets managed.

—Peter Drucker

Actionable Tip: Start a habit tracker. This could be a simple calendar where you mark off each day you complete your habit, a journal or a digital app. The key is to have a consistent method to track your progress.

Setting Clear and Achievable Goals

One of the reasons people fail to stick to their habits is that their goals are too vague or overly ambitious. Clear, achievable goals make it easier to stay on track.

Example: John, a friend of mine, decided to start running. Instead of setting a goal to run a marathon immediately, he set a goal to run three times a week for 20 minutes. This manageable goal made it easier for him to build the habit without feeling overwhelmed.

Actionable Tip: Break down your ultimate goal into smaller, achievable steps. Focus on consistency rather than intensity. Celebrate each milestone as you progress towards your larger goal.

The Role of Routine and Structure

Creating a routine around your habits can make them easier to maintain. When habits are part of your daily schedule, they become automatic and less reliant on motivation.

Example: Mark Zuckerberg, the founder of Facebook, is known for his consistent daily routine. By structuring his day and minimizing decision fatigue (such as wearing the same type of clothes every day), he ensures that his habits and responsibilities are consistently managed.

> *Motivation is what gets you started.*
> *Habit is what keeps you going.*
>
> —Jim Ryun

Actionable Tip: Establish a daily routine that includes your habits. Try to perform them at the same time each day to build consistency. Over time, they will become an automatic part of your day.

Accountability and Support Systems

Having someone to hold you accountable can significantly increase your chances of sticking to your habits. Support from friends, family or a community can provide motivation and encouragement.

Example: When my sister decided to quit smoking, she enlisted the help of a friend who had successfully quit a year earlier. They checked in with each other daily, providing support and encouragement. This accountability made a significant difference in her journey.

> *Surround yourself with only people*
> *who are going to lift you higher.*
>
> —Oprah Winfrey

Actionable Tip: Share your goals with someone you trust. Regular check-ins with an accountability partner can help you stay committed and motivated. Consider joining a group or community that shares similar goals.

Anticipating Obstacles and Planning Ahead

Life is unpredictable, and obstacles are inevitable. Anticipating potential challenges and planning how to deal with them can help you stay on track.

Example: Olympic swimmer Michael Phelps visualized potential obstacles in his races and mentally rehearsed how he would overcome them. This mental preparation helped him stay focused and resilient during competitions.

> *By failing to prepare, you are preparing to fail.*
>
> —Benjamin Franklin

Actionable Tip: Identify potential obstacles that could disrupt your habits. Plan ahead for how you will handle these challenges. Having a plan in place can help you navigate setbacks more effectively.

The Importance of Flexibility

While consistency is crucial, it's also important to be flexible. Life is dynamic, and sometimes you need to adapt your habits to fit changing circumstances.

Example: My friend Alex started a daily meditation habit but found it difficult to maintain when he travelled for work. Instead of abandoning the habit, he adapted by meditating for shorter periods or at different times of the day. This flexibility allowed him to stay consistent even with a changing schedule.

> *Blessed are the flexible, for they*
> *shall not be bent out of shape.*
>
> —Michael McGriffy, M.D.

Actionable Tip: Be prepared to adapt your habits as needed. If you miss a session or encounter an obstacle, don't be too hard on yourself. Adjust your approach and keep moving forward.

Bouncing Back Quickly After Missing a Habit

Missing a habit is inevitable, but what matters is how you respond. Developing a resilient mindset and strategies to bounce back quickly can help you maintain long-term success.

Example: J.K. Rowling faced numerous rejections before her Harry Potter series was published. Despite the setbacks, she persisted and continued writing. Her resilience paid off, leading to one of the most successful book series of all time.

> *It's not whether you get knocked down;*
> *it's whether you get up.*
>
> —Vince Lombardi

Actionable Tip: When you miss a habit, don't dwell on the failure. Reflect on what caused the slip and how you can prevent it in the future. Get back on track as soon as possible and focus on your progress rather than perfection.

The Power of Positive Self-Talk

How you talk to yourself can significantly impact your ability to maintain your habits. Positive self-talk can boost your confidence and resilience.

Example: Muhammad Ali was known for his positive affirmations. He famously said, "I am the greatest," long before he became the world champion. This positive self-talk helped him build the confidence and mindset necessary for success.

The words you speak become the house you live in.

—Hafiz

Actionable Tip: Practice positive self-talk. When you face setbacks, remind yourself of your strengths and capabilities. Encourage yourself as you would a friend. This positive mindset can help you stay motivated and resilient.

Reflecting on Your Progress

Regular reflection on your progress can help you stay on track and make necessary adjustments. It's an opportunity to celebrate your successes and learn from your challenges.

Example: Atul Gawande, a renowned surgeon and author, uses reflection to improve his skills. After each surgery, he takes time to review what went well and what could be improved. This practice of reflection has helped him continually enhance his performance.

Follow effective action with quiet reflection. From the quiet reflection will come even more effective action.

—Peter Drucker

Actionable Tip: Set aside time each week to reflect on your habits. Consider what is working well and what could be improved. Use this reflection to adjust your approach and stay aligned with your goals.

Celebrating Small Wins

Celebrating small wins can provide motivation and a sense of achievement. Recognizing and rewarding your progress, no matter how small, reinforces positive behaviour.

Example: My colleague Lisa set a goal to write a novel. Instead of focusing solely on the final product, she celebrated each completed chapter with a small reward, like a dinner out or a new book. These small celebrations kept her motivated and excited about her progress.

> *Little by little, one travels far.*
>
> —J.R.R. Tolkien

Actionable Tip: Celebrate your small wins. Acknowledge and reward your progress, no matter how minor it may seem. This positive reinforcement can keep you motivated and committed to your habits.

Creating a Habit-Friendly Environment

Your environment can significantly influence your ability to maintain habits. Creating a habit-friendly environment can reduce friction and make it easier to stay on track.

Example: James Clear, author of *Atomic Habits*, shares the story of how he transformed his environment to support his writing habit. He eliminated distractions from his workspace and created a dedicated writing area. This environment made it easier for him to focus and write consistently.

Environment is stronger than willpower.

—Paramahansa Yogananda

Actionable Tip: Assess your environment and make changes to support your habits. Remove distractions, create dedicated spaces for your habits and ensure that your environment aligns with your goals.

Using Technology to Your Advantage

In today's digital age, technology can be a powerful ally in habit formation. Various apps and tools can help you track, remind and reinforce your habits.

Example: Jerry Seinfeld uses a simple method called "Don't Break the Chain" to stay consistent with his writing. He marks an 'X' on a calendar for every day he writes. The visual chain of 'X's motivates him to keep going. Nowadays, there are apps like Habitica and HabitBull that can help you create similar tracking systems.

Success is the sum of small efforts,
repeated day in and day out.

—Robert Collier

Actionable Tip: Explore habit-tracking apps that suit your needs. Set reminders and use automated systems to help you stick to your habits. The less you have to think about it, the more likely you'll follow through.

Embracing the Power of Community

Being part of a community can provide a sense of belonging and shared purpose. Communities offer support, encouragement and accountability, making it easier to maintain your habits.

Example: CrossFit is known for its strong community aspect. Members support and motivate each other, creating an environment where individuals are more likely to stick to their fitness routines. The sense of community helps members stay committed and accountable.

> *Alone we can do so little; together we can do so much.*
>
> —Helen Keller

Actionable Tip: Join a community or group that shares your goals. Participate in activities, share your progress and support others. The sense of belonging and shared purpose can keep you motivated and on track.

Building a Resilient Mindset

Resilience is the ability to bounce back from setbacks. Developing a resilient mindset is crucial for maintaining habits in the long term.

Example: Thomas Edison faced numerous failures before successfully inventing the electric light bulb. He famously said, "I have not failed. I've just found 10,000 ways that won't work." His resilience and persistence led to his ultimate success.

> *Our greatest glory is not in never falling,*
> *but in rising every time we fall.*
>
> —Confucius

Actionable Tip: Embrace a growth mindset. View setbacks as learning opportunities rather than failures. Develop resilience by staying focused on your goals and adapting your approach as needed.

Conclusion: The Five-Point Takeaway

1. **Track and Reflect:** Keep a habit tracker and regularly reflect on your progress.
2. **Set Clear Goals and Routine:** Break down your goals into achievable steps and establish a consistent routine.
3. **Utilize Accountability and Community:** Share your goals with someone and join a supportive community.
4. **Celebrate Small Wins and Adapt:** Acknowledge your progress and be flexible in adapting your habits.
5. **Develop Resilience:** Embrace setbacks as learning opportunities and maintain a positive, resilient mindset.

By implementing these strategies, you can ensure that your habits stay on track and bounce back quickly after setbacks. Remember, the journey of habit formation is ongoing, but with the right approach, you can achieve lasting success.

15

Breaking the Cycle: Ensuring Bad Habits Don't Return

We've all been there—trying to kick a bad habit, feeling motivated and optimistic, only to find ourselves slipping back into the same old routines. The cycle can feel endless and frustrating. But don't worry; you're not alone, and there are ways to break free from this pattern. In this chapter, we'll explore practical strategies to ensure bad habits don't return, track our progress with good habits and find motivators to keep us on the right path. Let's dive in!

Understanding the Nature of Habits

Before we jump into the how-to's, let's understand what habits are. Habits are behaviours that have become automatic due to repetition. They are your brain's way of saving energy by putting certain actions on autopilot. This is great when it comes to good habits like brushing your teeth, but not so great for bad habits like biting your nails or procrastinating.

Why Bad Habits Stick

Bad habits often stick because they provide some kind of immediate reward or relief, even if it's temporary. For example, smoking might relieve stress momentarily, or scrolling through social media can be a quick distraction from work. Understanding the immediate reward is crucial in breaking the habit because it helps us find healthier alternatives.

Strategies to Ensure Bad Habits Don't Return

1. Identify Triggers and Replace the Routine

A key step in breaking bad habits is identifying what triggers them. For instance, if you snack mindlessly while watching TV, the trigger might be boredom or the TV itself. Once you've identified the trigger, you can replace the routine with a healthier one.

Anecdote: Sarah loved to munch on chips while binge-watching her favourite shows. She realized her snacking was more about the action than hunger. So, she replaced chips with a bowl of mixed nuts and fruits. Over time, this became her new routine, helping her avoid unhealthy snacking.

Prescription: Keep a diary for a week, noting down when and where your bad habit occurs. Look for patterns and identify triggers. Once identified, brainstorm healthier routines to replace the bad habit.

2. Use the "If-Then" Strategy

The "If-Then" strategy involves planning how to deal with situations that might trigger your bad habit. For example, "If I feel the urge to smoke, then I will chew gum instead."

Example: Mark wanted to quit smoking. He used the "If-Then" strategy effectively: "If I feel the urge to smoke, then I will take a walk around the block." This simple yet powerful technique helped him resist the urge to smoke.

Prescription: Write down at least three "If-Then" scenarios for your bad habit. Practice these scenarios mentally so you're prepared when the trigger arises.

3. Make it Harder to Engage in Bad Habits

Increase the friction or effort required to engage in the bad habit. The harder it is to do, the less likely you'll do it.

Anecdote: Emily had a habit of checking her phone constantly while studying. To combat this, she started leaving her phone in another room. The extra effort to get up and fetch her phone reduced her phone-checking habit significantly.

Prescription: Identify ways to increase the effort required for your bad habit. For example, if you want to reduce social media use, log out of your accounts after each session and remove the apps from your home screen.

4. Surround Yourself with Positive Influences

Your environment plays a crucial role in habit formation. Surround yourself with people who encourage and support your good habits and discourage bad ones.

Example: John wanted to quit drinking alcohol. He joined a support group and started spending more time with friends who enjoyed alcohol-free activities. The positive influence and support helped him stay on track.

Prescription: Seek out supportive communities, whether in person or online. Join groups or clubs that align with your goals and spend more time with people who support your positive changes.

5. Practice Mindfulness and Stress Management

Many bad habits are coping mechanisms for stress and anxiety. Practicing mindfulness and stress management techniques can help you deal with the underlying issues rather than resorting to bad habits.

Anecdote: Lisa had a habit of stress-eating. She started practicing mindfulness meditation and deep breathing exercises. Over time, she found herself reaching for healthy snacks and dealing with stress more effectively.

Prescription: Incorporate mindfulness practices into your daily routine. This could include meditation, deep breathing exercises or even mindful walking. Identify stressors and develop healthier coping mechanisms.

Tracking Progress with Good Habits

1. Set Clear Goals and Milestones

Define what success looks like for your good habit. Set clear, achievable goals and break them down into smaller milestones. This makes tracking progress easier and keeps you motivated.

Example: Emma wanted to run a marathon. She set clear milestones: running 5K, 10K, half-marathon and finally, the full marathon. Tracking her progress through these milestones kept her motivated and on track.

Prescription: Break down your ultimate goal into smaller, manageable milestones. Celebrate each milestone as a significant achievement on your journey.

2. Keep a Habit Journal

Write down your goals, daily progress and any challenges you face. A habit journal helps you reflect on your journey and stay accountable.

Anecdote: Michael started a habit journal to track his progress in learning the guitar. He noted down his practice sessions, what he learned each day and any difficulties he faced. Looking back at his entries, he could see his progress, which kept him motivated.

Prescription: Start a habit journal today. Dedicate a few minutes each evening to write about your progress, challenges and feelings about your habit journey.

3. Use Habit-Tracking Apps

There are many apps available that can help you track your habits. These apps provide reminders, track your progress and often have community support.

Example: Sarah used a habit-tracking app to monitor her water intake. The app sent her reminders and tracked her daily consumption, helping her stay hydrated and develop a consistent habit.

Prescription: Research and choose a habit-tracking app that suits your needs. Set up your goals and reminders, and regularly check your progress through the app.

4. Celebrate Small Wins

Celebrate your progress, no matter how small. Acknowledging your achievements boosts your motivation and reinforces positive behaviour.

Anecdote: Tom was trying to build a reading habit. He set a goal to read 20 pages a day. Every week, he celebrated his progress with a small treat, like a favourite snack or a movie night. These small celebrations kept him motivated and turned reading into a joyful habit.

Prescription: Set up a reward system for your milestones. Ensure the rewards are meaningful to you and celebrate your progress regularly.

Finding Motivators and Accountability

1. Find an Accountability Partner

Having someone hold you accountable can make a huge difference. Choose someone who supports your goals and will check in on your progress regularly.

Example: Jenny and her friend Lisa decided to hold each other accountable for their fitness goals. They shared their workout plans, checked in daily and encouraged each other. This mutual support helped them stay consistent.

Prescription: Identify a friend or family member who can be your accountability partner. Set up regular check-ins and support each other's goals.

2. Join a Community or Support Group

Joining a group of people with similar goals can provide a sense of community and accountability. Support groups offer encouragement, share tips and help you stay committed.

Anecdote: David joined an online community for aspiring writers. The group had weekly check-ins, writing challenges and shared resources. The sense of belonging and support helped him stay motivated and improve his writing habits.

Prescription: Look for online or local communities related to your goals. Participate actively and engage with the group to build a support network.

3. Use Visual Reminders

Visual reminders can keep your goals at the top of your mind. Use sticky notes, vision boards or apps that send reminders to keep you focused on your habits.

Example: Clara wanted to drink more water. She placed sticky notes with motivational quotes and reminders around her house and office. These visual cues kept her on track and made it easier to remember her goal.

Prescription: Create visual reminders for your goals. Place them in areas where you spend a lot of time to keep your goals in sight and in mind.

4. Reward Yourself

Rewards can be a powerful motivator. Set up a reward system for when you achieve certain milestones. Make sure the rewards are meaningful to you.

Anecdote: Mark wanted to build a habit of exercising daily. He promised himself a new pair of running shoes after a month of consistent workouts. The anticipation of the reward kept him motivated and committed to his fitness routine.

Prescription: Establish a system of rewards for yourself. Link your rewards to specific milestones and ensure they are significant enough to keep you motivated.

Ensuring You Don't Slip Back

1. Reflect on Your Why

Always remind yourself why you wanted to change the habit in the first place. Reflecting on your reasons can renew your commitment and keep you focused.

Example: Emily wanted to quit smoking to improve her health and be a better role model for her children. Whenever she felt the urge to smoke, she reminded herself of these reasons, which strengthened her resolve.

Prescription: Regularly write down and review the reasons behind your goal. Keep these reasons visible as a constant reminder of your commitment.

2. Learn from Setbacks

Setbacks are a natural part of the journey. Instead of getting discouraged, view them as learning opportunities. Analyze what went wrong and how you can prevent it in the future.

John had a setback when he started drinking again after six months of sobriety. Instead of giving up, he reflected on the triggers that led to his relapse and developed a new plan to address them. This resilience helped him get back on track and stay committed.

Prescription: When setbacks occur, take time to reflect and analyze. Develop new strategies to address the issues and prevent future setbacks.

3. Develop a Routine

A consistent routine can help you maintain good habits and prevent bad ones from creeping back in. Structure your day to include time for your positive habits.

Example: Lisa developed a morning routine that included meditation, a healthy breakfast and a quick workout. This routine set a positive tone for her day and made it easier to stick to her good habits.

Prescription: Design a daily routine that incorporates your good habits. Stick to this routine as closely as possible to reinforce your positive behaviours.

4. Stay Flexible and Adapt

Life is unpredictable, and rigidity can lead to frustration. Stay flexible and adapt your habits to fit different circumstances. This flexibility will help you maintain your habits even when life gets hectic.

Michael's work schedule changed, making it difficult for him to practice guitar at his usual time. Instead of giving up, he adapted by finding a new practice time that fit his new schedule. This flexibility allowed him to continue improving his skills without interruption.

Prescription: Be prepared to adapt your habits when life changes. Flexibility ensures that you can maintain your good habits regardless of your circumstances.

Conclusion

Breaking the cycle of bad habits and ensuring you stay on track with good ones is a journey that requires patience, persistence and a bit of strategy. By understanding the nature of habits, identifying triggers, setting clear goals and finding motivators, you can create lasting positive change. Remember, setbacks are part of the process, but with the right mindset and tools, you can overcome them and continue moving forward. Celebrate your progress, no matter how small, and keep pushing towards a healthier, happier you.

In the end, it's all about progress, not perfection. Stay committed, stay flexible, and most importantly, be kind to yourself. You've got this!

Prescriptions and Takeaways

1. Identify Triggers and Replace the Routine:
   - Keep a diary for a week, noting down when and where your bad habit occurs.
   - Look for patterns and identify triggers.
   - Brainstorm healthier routines to replace the bad habit.
2. Use the "If-Then" Strategy:
   - Write down at least three "If-Then" scenarios for your bad habit.
   - Practice these scenarios mentally so you're prepared when the trigger arises.
3. Make it Harder to Engage in Bad Habits:
   - Identify ways to increase the effort required to fix your bad habits.
   - Log out of social media accounts after each session and remove the apps from your home screen.
4. Surround Yourself with Positive Influences:
   - Seek out supportive communities, whether in person or online.
   - Join groups or clubs that align with your goals.
5. Practice Mindfulness and Stress Management:
   - Incorporate mindfulness practices into your daily routine.
   - Identify stressors and develop healthier coping mechanisms.

6. Set Clear Goals and Milestones:
   - Break down your ultimate goal into smaller, manageable milestones.
   - Celebrate each milestone as a significant achievement on your journey.
7. Keep a Habit Journal:
   - Start a habit journal and dedicate a few minutes each evening to write about your progress, challenges and feelings.
8. Use Habit-Tracking Apps:
   - Research and choose a habit-tracking app that suits your needs.
   - Set up your goals and reminders, and regularly check your progress.
9. Celebrate Small Wins:
   - Set up a reward system for your milestones.
   - Ensure the rewards are meaningful to you and celebrate your progress regularly.
10. Find an Accountability Partner:
    - Identify a friend or family member who can be your accountability partner.
    - Set up regular check-ins and support each other's goals.
11. Join a Community or Support Group:
    - Look for online or local communities related to your goals.
    - Participate actively and engage with the group to build a support network.
12. Use Visual Reminders:
    - Create visual reminders for your goals.
    - Place them in areas where you spend a lot of time to keep your goals in sight and in mind.

13. Reward Yourself:
    - Establish a system of rewards for yourself.
    - Link your rewards to specific milestones and ensure they are significant enough to keep you motivated.
14. Reflect on Your Why:
    - Regularly write down and review the reasons behind your goal.
    - Keep these reasons visible as a constant reminder of your commitment.
15. Learn from Setbacks:
    - When setbacks occur, take time to reflect and analyze.
    - Develop new strategies to address the issues and prevent future setbacks.
16. Develop a Routine:
    - Design a daily routine that incorporates your good habits.
    - Stick to this routine as closely as possible to reinforce your positive behaviours.
17. Stay Flexible and Adapt:
    - Be prepared to adapt your habits when life changes.
    - Flexibility ensures that you can maintain your good habits regardless of your circumstances.

By following these strategies and tips, you'll be well on your way to breaking bad habits, staying on track with good ones, and finding the motivation you need to keep going. Happy habit-forming!

16

Your Perfect Habit Match: What Your Genes and Personality Says

Have you ever tried to pick up a new habit, only to find it just doesn't stick? Maybe you've started running because everyone says it's great, but you quickly realize you dread every step. Or perhaps you've tried to journal daily, but it feels more like a chore than a joy. What if I told you that the key to developing lasting habits might lie in understanding your unique personality, your genes and your physical and emotional needs? In this chapter, we'll explore how to identify habits that suit you, the role of genetics in habit formation and how to cultivate habits that align with your personality. Ready to dive in? Let's go!

Understanding the Role of Genes in Habit Formation

Are Habits Written in Our DNA?

First things first: do our genes determine our habits? The answer is both yes and no. Genetics can influence certain behaviours and tendencies, making you more predisposed to some habits over others. For instance, studies have shown that genetics can impact traits like risk-taking, impulsivity and even how your body responds to physical exercise.

Anecdote: Take Laura, for example. She comes from a family of night owls. No matter how hard she tried, waking up early never felt natural to her. After learning about chronotypes and genetic predispositions to sleep patterns, she embraced her natural tendency and adjusted her schedule to be more productive in the evening. Instead of fighting her genetic makeup, she worked with it.

Prescription: Consider taking a genetic test that provides insights into your tendencies, such as whether you're naturally more inclined to be a night owl or an early bird. This can help you align your habits with your natural inclinations.

The Influence of Genetics on Physical Activity

Your genetic makeup can also influence how your body responds to different types of physical activity. Some people are naturally more inclined to excel in endurance activities, while others might be better suited for strength training.

Example: Ben always struggled with long-distance running but excelled in weightlifting. After reading about genetic predispositions, he realized his body was more suited for strength-based activities. He shifted his focus to weight training and found a routine that felt rewarding and sustainable.

Prescription: Pay attention to how your body feels during different types of exercise. Consider getting a genetic fitness test to understand your predispositions better and tailor your workouts accordingly.

Identifying Habits That Suit You

1. Reflect on Your Personality and Preferences

Understanding your personality is crucial in identifying habits that will stick. Are you introverted or extroverted? Do you prefer routine or spontaneity? Are you more analytical or creative? These traits can significantly influence which habits are suitable for you.

Anecdote: Sam, an extrovert, found it challenging to stick to a solo exercise routine. He thrived on social interaction and quickly grew bored running alone. When he joined a group fitness class, he found the social environment motivating and enjoyable, making it easier to stick to his fitness goals.

Prescription: Take a personality test, such as the Myers-Briggs Type Indicator (MBTI) or the Big Five Personality Traits test. Reflect on the results and think about how they align with your current habits and any new ones you want to develop.

2. Consider Your Lifestyle

Your current lifestyle plays a big role in determining which habits are sustainable. If you have a busy schedule, adopting a habit that requires significant time might not be practical. Instead, look for habits that fit seamlessly into your daily routine.

Anecdote: Jane, a busy mom of three, struggled to find time for a lengthy workout. Instead of trying to carve out an hour each day, she started incorporating short, 10-minute workouts throughout her day—doing squats while waiting for the microwave or stretching while helping with homework. These mini-sessions added up and were more manageable with her busy lifestyle.

Prescription: Analyze your daily schedule and identify small pockets of time where you can introduce new habits. This could be during your commute, while waiting in line or during commercial breaks.

3. Align Habits with Your Goals and Values

Habits that align with your personal goals and values are more likely to stick. Consider what's truly important to you and how a new habit can help you achieve those goals.

Anecdote: Tom valued sustainability and wanted to reduce his environmental footprint. Instead of feeling overwhelmed by drastic lifestyle changes, he started small by bringing reusable bags to the grocery store and gradually expanded to composting and reducing single-use plastics. These habits aligned with his values, making them easier to adopt and maintain.

Prescription: Write down your top five values and goals. Think about how new habits can support these and choose habits that align with what matters most to you.

Developing and Cultivating Habits that Align with Your Personality

1. Start Small and Build Gradually

One of the most effective ways to develop new habits is to start small and gradually build-up. This approach makes the habit less intimidating and more achievable.

Anecdote: John wanted to start meditating but found the idea of sitting still for 20 minutes daunting. He started with just one minute a day and gradually increased the time as he became more comfortable with the practice. Over time, he developed a consistent meditation habit that felt natural and enjoyable.

Prescription: Identify the smallest possible version of the habit you want to develop. Start with that and gradually increase the duration or intensity as you become more comfortable.

2. Pair New Habits with Existing Ones

Pairing a new habit with an existing one can make it easier to remember and stick to. This technique, known as habit stacking, leverages the power of your existing routines to support new behaviours.

Anecdote: Sarah wanted to start flossing daily but kept forgetting. She decided to pair flossing with her existing habit of brushing her teeth. By placing the floss right next to her toothbrush and committing to floss right after brushing, she successfully incorporated flossing into her daily routine.

Prescription: Look at your current habits and find opportunities to stack new habits onto existing ones. For example, you could meditate after your morning coffee or do a quick workout right after brushing your teeth.

3. Use Positive Reinforcement

Positive reinforcement can be a powerful motivator in developing new habits. Reward yourself for sticking to your habit to reinforce the behaviour.

Anecdote: Lisa loved reading but found it hard to make time for it. She decided to reward herself with a small piece of chocolate every time she finished a chapter. This simple reward made reading even more enjoyable and helped her establish a regular reading habit.

Prescription: Choose a small reward for yourself each time you complete your new habit. Make sure the reward is something you enjoy and look forward to.

4. Make Habits Enjoyable

If a habit feels like a chore, you're less likely to stick with it. Find ways to make your habits enjoyable and fun.

Anecdote: Mike wanted to get more active but hated the gym. He discovered he loved dancing and started attending dance classes instead. Because he enjoyed the activity, he found it easy to stick with and looked forward to each class.

Prescription: Experiment with different activities until you find one you genuinely enjoy. Whether it's a different form of exercise, a new hobby or a creative project, enjoyment is key to sustainability.

5. Track Your Progress

Tracking your progress helps you stay accountable and motivated. It allows you to see how far you've come and keeps you focused on your goals.

Anecdote: Emma used a habit-tracking app to monitor her progress in learning Spanish. Seeing her daily streak grow motivated her to keep practicing, and she enjoyed the sense of accomplishment that came with each new milestone.

Prescription: Use a habit-tracking app or a simple journal to record your progress. Make it a daily routine to check in and celebrate your achievements.

The Emotional Aspect of Habit Formation

1. Understand Your Emotional Triggers

Emotions play a significant role in habit formation. Understanding your emotional triggers can help you develop habits that support your emotional well-being.

Anecdote: Rachel found herself reaching for junk food whenever she felt stressed. By recognizing this emotional trigger, she started practicing deep breathing exercises whenever she felt stressed instead. This helped her manage her stress in a healthier way and reduced her reliance on junk food.

Prescription: Pay attention to how you feel before engaging in a habit. If you notice a pattern, find healthier ways to address those emotions. For example, practice mindfulness or talk to a friend instead of reaching for comfort food.

2. Cultivate Self-Compassion

Being hard on yourself for not sticking to a habit can be counterproductive. Cultivating self-compassion can help you stay motivated and resilient.

Anecdote: Mark used to beat himself up whenever he missed a workout, which made him feel demotivated. He started practicing self-compassion by acknowledging that everyone has off days and focusing on getting back on track. This shift in mindset helped him stay consistent and enjoy his fitness journey more.

Prescription: Practice self-compassion by speaking to yourself as you would to a friend. If you miss a habit, acknowledge it without judgment and focus on your next opportunity to practice it.

3. Seek Support and Connection

Support from others can significantly impact your ability to stick to new habits. Connecting with people who share your goals can provide encouragement and accountability.

Anecdote: Linda wanted to quit smoking but found it difficult to do alone. She joined a support group where she connected with others going through the same journey. The support and encouragement she received from the group made a huge difference in her ability to stay smoke-free.

Prescription: Seek out support groups, communities or friends who share your goals.

Share your journey with them and offer support in return.

Aligning Habits with Your Physical Needs

1. Listen to Your Body

Your body knows best when it comes to physical habits. Pay attention to how different activities make you feel and adjust accordingly.

Anecdote: James pushed himself to run every day because he thought it was the best way to stay fit. However, he often felt exhausted and experienced frequent injuries. He started listening to his body and incorporated a mix of running, yoga and strength training instead. This balanced approach made him feel more energized and reduced his risk of injury.

Prescription: Tune into your body's signals. If a physical activity leaves you feeling drained or in pain, explore alternative forms of exercise that you enjoy and that suit your physical needs.

2. Consider Your Energy Levels

Your energy levels can fluctuate throughout the day, and aligning your habits with these natural rhythms can enhance your success.

Anecdote: Mia noticed she had the most energy in the morning, so she scheduled her workouts first thing in the day. By aligning her exercise routine with her peak energy levels, she found it easier to stay consistent and enjoyed her workouts more.

Prescription: Track your energy levels throughout the day for a week. Identify when you feel most energetic and schedule your most important habits during those times.

3. Adapt to Your Environment

Your environment can significantly impact your ability to maintain habits. Creating a supportive environment can make it easier to stick to your habits.

Anecdote: Alex wanted to eat healthier but found it hard to resist junk food at home. He reorganized his kitchen, placing healthy snacks at eye level and moving junk food out of sight. This simple change in his environment made it easier to make healthier choices.

Prescription: Modify your environment to support your habits. Arrange your space so that healthy choices are convenient and unhealthy ones are less accessible.

Practical Steps to Identify and Cultivate Habits

Step 1: Self-Assessment

Start with a thorough self-assessment. Reflect on your personality, lifestyle, goals and values. Consider what habits you've successfully maintained in the past and why they worked for you.

Exercise: Write down five habits you've tried to develop in the past. Identify which ones stuck and which ones didn't. Reflect on the reasons behind their success or failure.

Step 2: Experiment and Reflect

Try different habits on a small scale and see how they feel. Reflect on your experiences and adjust accordingly.

Exercise: Choose one new habit to try for a week. At the end of the week, reflect on how it felt, any challenges you faced and whether it's a habit you want to continue.

Step 3: Set Clear Goals

Define what you want to achieve with your new habit. Set clear, achievable goals and milestones to keep you motivated.

Exercise: Write down your habit goal and break it into smaller milestones. For example, if your goal is to read more, start with a goal of reading one book a month and increase gradually.

Step 4: Find Support

Seek out support from friends, family or communities. Share your goals and ask for their encouragement and accountability.

Exercise: Identify one person you trust and share your habit goal with them. Ask them to check in with you regularly and offer support.

Step 5: Track and Adjust

Tracking your progress and being flexible are crucial for long-term success. If a habit isn't working for you, don't be afraid to adjust or try something new.

Exercise: Use a journal or app to track your progress. Reflect on your journey regularly and make adjustments as needed.

Real-Life Examples of Habit Success

Example 1: The Power of Community Support

Anecdote: Jenny wanted to improve her public speaking skills but felt terrified at the thought of speaking in front of an audience. She joined a local Toastmasters club where she found a supportive community of individuals working towards the same goal. The encouragement and constructive feedback she received helped her grow more confident and significantly improve her public speaking abilities.

Takeaway: The support of a community can provide the encouragement and accountability needed to develop new habits, especially when facing challenging goals.

Example 2: Adapting to Personal Preferences

Anecdote: Kevin always struggled with traditional forms of exercise like running or going to the gym. However, he loved playing basketball. He started playing pickup games at a local court several times a week. This not only kept him physically active but also made exercise something he genuinely looked forward to.

Takeaway: Aligning habits with personal interests and preferences can transform challenging tasks into enjoyable activities, increasing the likelihood of long-term adherence.

Example 3: Leveraging Technology for Habit Tracking

Maria wanted to improve her sleep habits but found it difficult to go to bed early. She started using a sleep-tracking app that provided insights into her sleep patterns and offered personalized tips for better sleep hygiene. By following the app's recommendations and tracking her progress, she gradually developed healthier sleep habits.

Takeaway: Utilizing technology for habit tracking and personalized advice can provide valuable insights and support for developing and maintaining new habits.

Example 4: Integrating Mindfulness into Daily Routine

David often felt overwhelmed by work stress and wanted to find a way to manage it better. He started incorporating short mindfulness exercises into his daily routine, such as deep breathing during lunch breaks and a brief meditation before bed. These small changes helped him manage stress more effectively and improved his overall well-being.

Takeaway: Integrating mindfulness practices into daily routines can provide powerful benefits for managing stress and supporting emotional well-being.

Example 5: Creating a Reward System

Hannah was determined to write a book but found it difficult to stay motivated. She created a reward system where she treated herself to a small reward after completing each chapter. This system provided the motivation she needed to stay on track and eventually complete her book.

Takeaway: Establishing a reward system can enhance motivation and provide positive reinforcement, making it easier to stick to new habits.

Conclusion

Finding habits that suit you is a journey of self-discovery. By understanding your genetic predispositions, personality and physical and emotional needs, you can develop and cultivate habits that align with who you are. Remember, the key to lasting habits is to start small, be flexible and enjoy the process. Celebrate your progress, seek support and always listen to your body and mind. Happy habit-forming!

Perceptions and Takeaways

1. Understand Your Genetic Tendencies:
    - Consider taking a genetic test to gain insights into your natural inclinations and tailor your habits accordingly.
    - Pay attention to how your body responds to different types of physical activity and adjust your exercise routines based on these responses.
2. Reflect on Your Personality and Preferences:
    - Take personality tests like the MBTI or Big Five to understand your traits better.
    - Align your habits with your personality to increase the likelihood of success.
3. Adapt to Your Lifestyle:
    - Analyze your daily schedule to find small pockets of time for new habits.
    - Choose habits that fit seamlessly into your existing routines to make them more sustainable.
4. Align Habits with Your Goals and Values:
    - Identify your top five values and goals and select habits that support these.

- Reflect on how new habits can help you achieve what matters most to you.
5. Start Small and Build Gradually:
    - Begin with the smallest possible version of a habit and gradually increase its intensity or duration.
    - Focus on making the habit less intimidating and more achievable.
6. Pair New Habits with Existing Ones:
    - Use habit stacking to pair new habits with existing routines.
    - Look for opportunities to integrate new behaviours into your daily life.
7. Use Positive Reinforcement:
    - Choose small rewards for completing new habits to reinforce the behaviour.
    - Make sure the rewards are something you enjoy and look forward to.
8. Make Habits Enjoyable:
    - Experiment with different activities until you find ones you genuinely enjoy.
    - Focus on enjoyment to increase the likelihood of long-term adherence.
9. Track Your Progress:
    - Use habit-tracking apps or journals to record your progress.
    - Make tracking a daily routine and celebrate your achievements.
10. Understand Your Emotional Triggers:
    - Pay attention to your emotions before engaging in a habit and find healthier ways to address them.
    - Practice mindfulness or talk to a friend to manage emotional triggers.

11. Cultivate Self-Compassion:
    - Speak to yourself with kindness and understanding, especially when you miss a habit.
    - Focus on getting back on track without judgment.
12. Seek Support and Connection:
    - Connect with support groups, communities or friends who share your goals.
    - Share your journey and offer support to others.
13. Listen to Your Body:
    - Tune into your body's signals and adjust physical activities based on how you feel.
    - Explore alternative forms of exercise that suit your physical needs.
14. Consider Your Energy Levels:
    - Track your energy levels throughout the day and schedule important habits during peak times.
    - Align your routines with your natural rhythms for better success.
15. Adapt to Your Environment:
    - Modify your environment to support your habits.
    - Arrange your space to make healthy choices more convenient and unhealthy ones less accessible.

By following these strategies and insights, you'll be well on your way to identifying and cultivating habits that truly suit you. Embrace the journey and remember that the most important thing is to find what works best for you.

17

Beating Boredom: Staying Motivated and Fascinated with Good Habits

We've all been there—starting a new habit with tons of enthusiasm, only to find ourselves bored and unmotivated after a few weeks. Boredom can be a major obstacle to maintaining good habits, making it challenging to stay on track. But what if there were ways to keep the spark alive and continue with your habits without feeling like you're stuck in a rut? This chapter'll explore strategies to beat boredom, stay motivated and keep your habits fresh and exciting. Ready to reignite your passion for your good habits? Let's get started!

Understanding Boredom and Its Impact on Habits

Why We Get Bored

Boredom often sets in when a habit becomes too routine or repetitive. When the initial excitement wears off, the habit can start to feel mundane, leading to a lack of motivation. This is a natural part of the process, but it doesn't mean you must give up.

Anecdote: Jenny started running every morning with great enthusiasm. However, after a few months, she found herself dreading her runs. The same route, the same pace—it all felt monotonous. She realized she needed to shake things up to keep her motivation alive.

The Importance of Consistency

Consistency is key to forming lasting habits, but it's also where boredom can strike the hardest. Finding ways to maintain consistency without losing interest is crucial for long-term success.

Prescription: Reflect on your reasons for starting the habit in the first place. Remind yourself of the benefits and the progress you've made so far. This can help reignite your motivation and commitment.

Strategies to Beat Boredom and Stay Motivated

1. Add Variety to Your Routine

Mixing things up can make your habits feel fresh and exciting. Adding variety prevents your routine from becoming too predictable and keeps you engaged.

Anecdote: Mark loved cooking but found himself making the same dishes over and over again. To keep his passion for cooking alive, he started exploring cuisines from different cultures. Each week, he challenged himself to try a new recipe from a different country. This not only improved his cooking skills but also kept him excited about his culinary journey.

Prescription: Identify areas where you can introduce variety into your habits. For example, if you're exercising, try different workouts, change your running route or join a new fitness class.

2. Set New Challenges and Goals

Setting new challenges and goals can give you something to strive for and keep you motivated. Goals provide a sense of direction and purpose, making your habits feel more meaningful.

Anecdote: Lisa enjoyed painting but felt uninspired after a while. She decided to set a goal of creating a series of themed paintings—one month she focused on landscapes, the next on portraits. Each new challenge sparked her creativity and kept her excited about painting.

Prescription: Break your long-term goals into smaller, achievable milestones. Regularly set new challenges to keep things interesting and give yourself a sense of accomplishment.

3. Incorporate Fun and Playfulness

Adding an element of fun and playfulness to your habits can make them more enjoyable and less of a chore. When you're having fun, you're more likely to stick with it.

Anecdote: Tom found his daily workouts tedious. He decided to join a local sports league, playing soccer twice a week. The social interaction and competitive element made exercise fun, and he looked forward to his games.

Prescription: Think about how you can make your habits more fun. This could be through gamification, joining a group or adding a playful twist to your routine.

4. Track Your Progress and Celebrate Wins

Tracking your progress helps you see how far you've come, while celebrating wins reinforces positive behaviour. Both can boost your motivation and keep you on track.

Anecdote: Emma used a habit-tracking app to monitor her daily meditation practice. Seeing her progress visualized in the app kept her motivated, and she celebrated milestones with small rewards, like treating herself to a new book or a relaxing spa day.

Prescription: Use a habit-tracking app or journal to record your progress. Set up a reward system to celebrate milestones and keep your motivation high.

Keeping the Fascination Alive

1. Connect with Your Why

Reminding yourself why you started a habit in the first place can help you stay motivated. Connecting with your deeper purpose can reignite your passion and commitment.

Anecdote: Sarah started journaling to improve her mental health. Whenever she felt bored or unmotivated, she reread her initial journal entries and saw how much progress she had made. This reflection reminded her of the positive impact journaling had on her life and kept her going.

Prescription: Reflect regularly on your reasons for starting a habit. Write them down and revisit them whenever you feel your motivation waning.

2. Surround Yourself with Inspiration

Surrounding yourself with inspiration can help you stay fascinated with your habits. This could be through reading books, following influencers or joining communities that share your interests.

Anecdote: Mike wanted to improve his photography skills but felt uninspired. He started following professional photographers on social media and joined a local photography club. The community and constant flow of new ideas kept him motivated and inspired to continue improving.

Prescription: Find sources of inspiration that resonate with you. This could be online communities, books, podcasts or mentors who can provide new perspectives and ideas.

3. Embrace the Process, Not Just the Outcome

Focusing on the journey rather than just the end goal can help you stay engaged and motivated. Embrace the process and find joy in the small steps you take each day.

Anecdote: John wanted to learn guitar but found it frustrating when he didn't progress as quickly as he'd hoped. He shifted his focus from just wanting to master songs to enjoying the learning process. Practicing became more enjoyable when he appreciated each small improvement.

Prescription: Celebrate the small wins and enjoy the process. Focus on the daily practice and the progress you're making, rather than just the end result.

4. Make It Social

Sharing your habits with others can add a new dimension of fun and accountability. When you involve others, you create a sense of community and shared purpose.

Anecdote: David wanted to read more but often found himself procrastinating. He joined a book club where members met weekly to discuss what they were reading. The social aspect and the accountability of having to discuss his progress kept him motivated to read regularly.

Prescription: Join groups or find friends who share your habits. Create challenges, share progress and support each other to keep things interesting and engaging.

Staying Consistent with Good Habits

1. Plan for Plateaus and Setbacks

Understand that plateaus and setbacks are a natural part of the journey. Planning for these can help you stay motivated and avoid getting discouraged.

Anecdote: Jane was making great progress with her fitness goals until she hit a plateau. Instead of getting frustrated, she adjusted her routine, sought advice from a trainer and stayed patient. Her persistence paid off, and she eventually broke through the plateau.

Prescription: Expect plateaus and setbacks as part of the process. When they happen, adjust your approach, seek support and stay patient.

2. Use Positive Self-Talk

Positive self-talk can boost your motivation and help you stay committed to your habits. Encourage yourself and focus on the progress you've made.

Anecdote: Emily struggled with negative self-talk, especially when she missed a day of her new habit. She started practicing positive affirmations and focusing on her achievements rather than her slip-ups. This shift in mindset helped her stay motivated and consistent.

Prescription: Practice positive self-talk and affirmations. Remind yourself of your progress and be kind to yourself when you encounter setbacks.

3. Create a Flexible Routine

Flexibility in your routine can help you maintain your habits even when life gets busy. Adapt your habits to fit different circumstances to stay consistent.

Anecdote: Alex loved practising yoga but often missed sessions when his schedule got hectic. He created a flexible routine that allowed for shorter, more frequent sessions. This adaptability helped him stay consistent and maintain his practice.

Prescription: Design a flexible routine that allows for adjustments based on your schedule. Incorporate shorter, more manageable versions of your habits to maintain consistency.

Revitalizing Old Habits

1. Revisit and Refresh Your Habits

Sometimes, habits need a little refresh to keep them exciting. Revisit your old habits and find new ways to make them engaging.

Anecdote: Linda enjoyed journaling but found it becoming monotonous. She decided to try different journaling techniques, like gratitude lists and creative writing prompts. This variety reinvigorated her passion for journaling.

Prescription: Look for ways to refresh your habits. Experiment with new techniques or approaches to keep things interesting.

2. Incorporate Learning and Growth

Continual learning and growth can keep your habits from

becoming stagnant. Challenge yourself to improve and learn new skills related to your habits.

Anecdote: Steve loved gardening but felt he had mastered the basics. He started learning about more advanced techniques, like hydroponics and organic farming. This new knowledge kept his gardening practice exciting and fulfilling.

Prescription: Seek opportunities for learning and growth within your habits. Take courses, read books or find mentors to expand your skills and knowledge.

3. Reflect and Adapt

Regular reflection can help you identify areas for improvement and adapt your habits to better suit your needs.

Anecdote: Karen was dedicated to her morning routine but felt it was becoming too rigid. She took time to reflect on what was working and what wasn't. She made adjustments, like incorporating more flexibility and variety, which made her routine more enjoyable and sustainable.

Prescription: Set aside time to regularly reflect on your habits. Identify what's working, what's not and make necessary adjustments to keep your habits effective and engaging.

Practical Steps to Maintain Fascination

Step 1: Regularly Reevaluate Your Habits

Take time to reevaluate your habits periodically. Assess whether they still align with your goals and interests.

Exercise: Set a monthly or quarterly reminder to reflect on your habits. Ask yourself if they still serve your goals and if there are ways to make them more exciting.

Step 2: Introduce Novelty

Introducing novelty can keep your habits fresh and engaging. Try new approaches or add elements of surprise to your routine.

Exercise: Identify one habit that feels monotonous and brainstorm ways to introduce novelty. This could be through new techniques, environments or challenges.

Step 3: Celebrate Progress

Celebrate your progress regularly to reinforce positive behaviour and keep your motivation high.

Exercise: Create a list of milestones for your habits and plan small celebrations for each one. Make these celebrations meaningful and enjoyable.

Step 4: Seek Feedback

Getting feedback from others can provide new perspectives and keep you motivated.

Exercise: Share your habits and goals with a friend or mentor. Ask for their feedback and suggestions on keeping things interesting and improving your routine.

Conclusion

Boredom is a natural part of the habit-forming process, but it doesn't have to derail your progress. By incorporating variety, setting new challenges and making your habits enjoyable, you can stay motivated and fascinated with your good habits. Remember to connect with your deeper purpose, seek inspiration and celebrate your progress. With these strategies, you'll be well-equipped to maintain your habits and keep them exciting and fulfilling. Happy habit-forming!

Perceptions and Takeaways

1. Add Variety to Your Routine:
   - Identify areas where you can introduce variety into your habits.
   - Explore new approaches to keep your routine fresh and exciting.
2. Set New Challenges and Goals:
   - Break your long-term goals into smaller, achievable milestones.
   - Regularly set new challenges to keep things interesting.
3. Incorporate Fun and Playfulness:
   - Think about how you can make your habits more fun.
   - Add playful elements to your routine to enhance enjoyment.
4. Track Your Progress and Celebrate Wins:
   - Use a habit-tracking app or journal to record your progress.
   - Set up a reward system to celebrate milestones and keep your motivation high.
5. Connect with Your Why:
   - Reflect regularly on your reasons for starting a habit.
   - Revisit your initial motivations to reignite your passion.
6. Surround Yourself with Inspiration:
   - Find sources of inspiration that resonate with you.
   - Join communities, read books, or follow influencers who share your interests.
7. Embrace the Process, Not Just the Outcome:

- Celebrate the small wins and enjoy the process.
- Focus on the daily practice and progress rather than just the end result.

8. Make It Social:
   - Share your habits with others to add a new dimension of fun and accountability.
   - Join groups or find friends who share your habits.
9. Plan for Plateaus and Setbacks:
   - Expect plateaus and setbacks as part of the process.
   - Adjust your approach and seek support when necessary.
10. Use Positive Self-Talk:
    - Practice positive self-talk and affirmations.
    - Focus on your progress and be kind to yourself when you encounter setbacks.
11. Create a Flexible Routine:
    - Design a flexible routine that allows for adjustments.
    - Incorporate shorter, more manageable versions of your habits to maintain consistency.
12. Revisit and Refresh Your Habits:
    - Look for ways to refresh your habits.
    - Experiment with new techniques or approaches to keep things interesting.
13. Incorporate Learning and Growth:
    - Seek opportunities for learning and growth within your habits.
    - Take courses, read books or find mentors to expand your skills and knowledge.
14. Reflect and Adapt:
    - Set aside time for regular reflection on your habits.
    - Identify what's working, what's not and make necessary adjustments.
15. Regularly Reevaluate Your Habits:

- Take time to reevaluate your habits periodically.
- Assess whether they still align with your goals and interests.

16. Introduce Novelty:
    - Identify one habit that feels monotonous and brainstorm ways to introduce novelty.
    - Try new approaches or add elements of surprise to your routine.
17. Celebrate Progress:
    - Create a list of milestones for your habits and plan small celebrations for each one.
    - Make these celebrations meaningful and enjoyable.
18. Seek Feedback:
    - Share your habits and goals with a friend or mentor.
    - Ask for their feedback and suggestions for keeping things interesting and improving your routine.

By following these strategies and insights, you'll be well on your way to beating boredom, staying motivated and maintaining your good habits. Embrace the journey, and remember that the most important thing is to find what works best for you. Happy habit-forming!

18

Flexibility Over Rigidity: Adapting Habits with Changing Times

We've all heard the saying, "Old habits die hard." While it's true that habits can be deeply ingrained, it's also important to recognize that our belief systems and habits shouldn't become prisons that limit our growth. The world around us is constantly evolving, and so should we. Clinging too tightly to outdated habits and rigid beliefs can lead to stagnation, whereas flexibility and adaptability are keys to thriving in changing times. In this chapter, we'll explore how to avoid becoming a slave to your belief systems and habits, how to adapt or adopt new habits as times change, and why flexibility is essential for continued growth and success. Let's get started!

The Pitfalls of Rigidity

Why We Cling to Beliefs and Habits

Beliefs and habits provide a sense of stability and predictability in our lives. They are the mental shortcuts our brains create to navigate the complexities of daily life. However, this can become a double-edged sword. When we cling too tightly to these routines and belief systems, we risk becoming inflexible and resistant to change.

Anecdote: Take Mark, for example. Mark had always believed in the traditional nine-to-five work schedule. When his company introduced flexible working hours, he resisted, convinced that the new system would lead to chaos and reduced productivity. However, he soon realized that his colleagues were thriving with the new schedule, finding better work-life balance and increased productivity. Mark's rigidity initially held him back, but once he adapted, he found that the flexibility actually improved his performance.

Prescription: Reflect on your own beliefs and habits. Identify any that might be outdated or no longer serve you well. Ask yourself if there are new ways to approach these areas that might better suit your current circumstances.

The Dangers of Inflexibility

Inflexibility can lead to stagnation, missed opportunities and increased stress. When we are unwilling to adapt, we might find ourselves out of sync with the changing world around us.

Anecdote: Sarah, a teacher, insisted on using traditional teaching methods despite her students' struggles to engage with the material. She ignored the growing body of evidence supporting interactive and technology-based learning. Her inflexibility not only affected her students' performance but also led to her own professional stagnation. When she finally embraced new teaching methods, her classroom became more dynamic and her students more engaged.

Prescription: Stay informed about new developments and be open to experimenting with new methods. Adaptation is a continuous process that requires an open mind and a willingness to step out of your comfort zone.

Embracing Change: Adapting Your Beliefs and Habits

1. Recognize the Need for Change

The first step in adapting your beliefs and habits is recognizing when they no longer serve you. This awareness often comes from reflection and feedback from others.

Anecdote: John prided himself on his punctuality and rigid schedule. However, he noticed that his inflexibility was causing friction with his colleagues and limiting his ability to collaborate effectively. After receiving feedback, John realized the need to be more adaptable. He started allowing some flexibility in his schedule, which improved his relationships and productivity.

Prescription: Regularly reflect on your habits and beliefs. Seek feedback from trusted friends, family or colleagues to gain new perspectives on areas where you might need to adapt.

2. Be Open to New Ideas and Perspectives

Openness to new ideas is crucial for growth. This means being willing to listen to others and consider alternative viewpoints.

Anecdote: Emily was a firm believer in traditional marketing techniques. However, as digital marketing started to dominate the industry, she realized that her old methods were becoming less effective. By attending workshops and seeking advice from younger colleagues, Emily learned to embrace social media marketing and saw her business flourish.

Prescription: Engage with diverse perspectives by reading, attending workshops and networking with people from different backgrounds. This exposure will help you stay current and open-minded.

3. Experiment with New Habits

Trying out new habits can be a fun and effective way to discover what works best for you in the current context. This experimentation helps you stay flexible and adaptable.

Anecdote: Lisa, a fitness enthusiast, was dedicated to her daily gym routine. When the pandemic hit and gyms closed, she initially felt lost. Instead of giving up, she experimented with home workouts, yoga and outdoor activities. This not only kept her fit but also introduced her to new forms of exercise that she enjoyed.

Prescription: Regularly try out new habits and activities. Even if they don't become permanent parts of your routine, they can provide valuable insights and keep things interesting.

4. Reflect and Adjust

Reflection is key to understanding what works and what doesn't. Regularly assessing your habits and making necessary adjustments helps you stay aligned with your goals and current reality.

Anecdote: Tom had a strict no-screen time policy before bed to improve his sleep. However, he realized that reading on his e-reader helped him unwind more than traditional books. By reflecting on what truly helped him relax, he adjusted his habit to include e-reading, which improved his sleep quality.

Prescription: Set aside time for regular reflection. Ask yourself what habits are working, which ones aren't and what adjustments might be necessary. This iterative process helps you stay flexible and effective.

Cultivating Flexibility: Why It's Essential

The Benefits of Being Flexible

Flexibility allows you to navigate life's uncertainties with ease. It helps you respond to changes positively, seize new opportunities and maintain a sense of balance.

Anecdote: David, a freelance writer, used to have a strict work schedule. However, he found it challenging to maintain when his clients' needs varied. By becoming more flexible with his work hours, he was able to better accommodate his clients, take on more projects and ultimately increase his income.

Prescription: Embrace flexibility as a core value. This doesn't mean abandoning structure altogether, but rather being willing to adapt your plans and routines as needed.

How Inflexibility Leads to Stagnation

Inflexibility can cause you to miss out on new opportunities and hinder your personal and professional growth. It can also lead to increased stress when things don't go as planned.

Anecdote: Karen, a project manager, insisted on using the same project management tools she had always used, despite her team's struggles with them. Her resistance to change caused frustration and inefficiency. When she finally adopted a more user-friendly tool, her team's productivity and morale improved significantly.

Prescription: Stay open to new tools, technologies and methods that can enhance your effectiveness. Regularly evaluate your current systems and be willing to make changes when better options are available.

Practical Steps to Adapt and Adopt New Habits

Step 1: Identify Areas for Change

Start by identifying the areas in your life where your current habits and beliefs may no longer be serving you well.

Exercise: Make a list of your daily habits and core beliefs. Reflect on each one and consider whether it aligns with your current goals and context. Identify any that may need to be adjusted or replaced.

Step 2: Seek Out New Information and Perspectives

Expand your horizons by seeking out new information and perspectives. This can help you stay current and open to change.

Exercise: Commit to reading books and articles or listening to podcasts on topics outside your usual interests. Engage in conversations with people who have different viewpoints to broaden your perspective.

Step 3: Experiment with New Habits

Once you've identified areas for change, start experimenting with new habits. Keep an open mind and be willing to try different approaches.

Exercise: Choose one habit to change or introduce each month. Track your progress and reflect on how it impacts your life. Adjust as needed based on your experiences.

Step 4: Reflect and Adjust

Regular reflection helps you assess what's working and what's not. Make it a habit to reflect and adjust your routines regularly.

Exercise: Set aside time each week for reflection. Use a journal to note down what's working, what isn't and any adjustments you need to make. This practice helps you stay flexible and aligned with your goals.

Real-Life Examples of Adaptability and Flexibility

Example 1: Adapting to Remote Work

Anecdote: When the pandemic forced many companies to switch to remote work, Susan initially struggled with the transition. She was used to the structure of the office environment and found it hard to stay productive at home. By experimenting with different setups, establishing a flexible routine and seeking advice from her colleagues, Susan adapted to remote work. She even enjoyed the flexibility it offered and became more productive than ever.

Takeaway: Flexibility and willingness to adapt to new circumstances can lead to increased productivity and satisfaction, even in challenging situations.

Example 2: Embracing New Technology

Anecdote: Michael, a small business owner, was hesitant to embrace digital marketing. He relied on traditional methods like print ads and word-of-mouth. However, as more of his competitors moved online, he realized he needed to adapt. He took a digital marketing course, experimented with social media advertising and revamped his website. These changes brought in new customers and significantly boosted his business.

Takeaway: Embracing new technologies and methods can open up new opportunities and help you stay competitive in a rapidly changing world.

Example 3: Shifting Career Paths

Anecdote: Anna had spent a decade working in finance but felt unfulfilled. She was passionate about environmental conservation but was afraid to make a career change. After much reflection and seeking advice, she decided to pursue her passion. She took courses in environmental science, volunteered with conservation organizations and eventually landed a job in the field. Her flexibility and willingness to adapt led to a more fulfilling and aligned career.

Takeaway: Being open to changing your career path can lead to greater fulfilment and alignment with your passions and values.

Takeaways: Practical Prescriptions for Flexibility and Adaptability

1. Reflect Regularly:
   - Make it a habit to reflect on your beliefs and habits. Identify which ones are no longer serving you and need to be adjusted or replaced.
   - Use a journal to track your reflections and progress. Regular reflection helps you stay aware of what's working and what isn't.
2. Seek Feedback:
   - Ask for feedback from trusted friends, family or colleagues. They can provide valuable insights and perspectives that you might not see.
   - Be open to constructive criticism and use it as a tool for growth.
3. Stay Informed:
   - Keep up with new developments and trends in your field and areas of interest. This helps you stay current and open to new ideas.

- Read books, attend workshops and engage with diverse perspectives to broaden your understanding.
4. Experiment and Adjust:
    - Regularly experiment with new habits and approaches. Don't be afraid to try something new, even if it feels uncomfortable at first.
    - Reflect on your experiments and make adjustments based on what you learn.
5. Embrace Flexibility:
    - Adopt flexibility as a core value. Be willing to adapt your plans and routines as needed to stay aligned with your goals and context.
    - Create flexible routines that allow for adjustments based on changing circumstances.
6. Connect with Your Why:
    - Regularly remind yourself of the reasons behind your habits and goals. This helps you stay motivated and aligned with your deeper purpose.
    - Reflect on your values and ensure that your habits and beliefs support them.
7. Stay Curious:
    - Cultivate a mindset of curiosity and openness. Approach new ideas and experiences with a sense of wonder and willingness to learn.
    - Ask questions, seek new experiences and continuously explore new avenues for growth.
8. Surround Yourself with Inspiration:
    - Engage with communities and individuals who inspire you. Surround yourself with positive influences that encourage growth and adaptability.
    - Seek out mentors and role models who embody flexibility and adaptability.

By following these strategies and insights, you'll be well-equipped to avoid becoming a slave to outdated beliefs and habits. Embrace flexibility, stay open to new ideas and continuously adapt to changing times. This approach will help you grow, thrive and find fulfilment in an ever-evolving world. Happy adapting!

19

Staying Motivated: How to Bounce Back When You Slip Up on Your Habits

We've all been there—starting with a new habit or routine full of enthusiasm, only to find ourselves slipping up somewhere along the way. It's easy to feel discouraged and think, "Why bother?" But here's the thing: setbacks are a natural part of the journey. What matters is how we respond to them. In this chapter, we'll explore how not to get demotivated when you can't follow your routine, how to bounce back and why being kind to yourself is crucial. Ready to learn how to stay on track without being too hard on yourself? Let's dive in!

Understanding Setbacks

Why We Slip Up

Before we delve into how to bounce back, let's understand why we slip up in the first place. Life is unpredictable, and no matter how well we plan, things can go awry. Stress, unexpected events, changes in routine and even sheer exhaustion can throw us off track.

Take Sarah, for example. She started a new habit of morning jogging. For a few weeks, everything went smoothly until she had to travel for work. The change in routine disrupted her habit, and she found it hard to get back on track once she returned. Sarah felt frustrated and demotivated, questioning if she should even bother trying again.

Prescription: Recognize that setbacks are normal and happen to everyone. Understanding this can help reduce the pressure you put on yourself.

How to Bounce Back from Setbacks

1. Acknowledge Your Feelings

It's natural to feel frustrated or disappointed when you slip up. Acknowledging these feelings is the first step towards moving past them.

Anecdote: Mark was on a roll with his new habit of daily meditation. One particularly busy week, he missed several days in a row. He felt guilty and started doubting his commitment. Instead of pushing these feelings aside, Mark acknowledged his frustration and gave himself permission to feel disappointed. This acknowledgment helped him process his emotions and prepare to start again.

Prescription: When you slip up, take a moment to acknowledge your feelings without judgement. Write them down if it helps, and remember that it's okay to feel disappointed.

2. Reflect on the Cause

Understanding why you slipped up can provide valuable insights and help you avoid similar setbacks in the future. Reflect on the circumstances that led to the lapse.

Anecdote: Emma missed her habit of writing daily because of a sudden influx of work. Reflecting on this, she realized that she needed to adjust her schedule to accommodate busy periods better. She decided to set aside shorter, more manageable writing sessions during hectic times.

Prescription: Reflect on what caused the setback. Was it a change in routine, unexpected events, or something else? Understanding the cause can help you find solutions and prevent future lapses.

3. Adjust Your Approach

Sometimes, a slight adjustment to your habit or routine can make it easier to stick with, even during challenging times. Flexibility is key to maintaining habits.

Anecdote: John loved his evening workouts, but family commitments often disrupted his routine. He decided to experiment with morning workouts instead. This adjustment made it easier for him to stay consistent, as there were fewer interruptions in the morning.

Prescription: If a habit isn't working with your current routine, try adjusting it. Experiment with different times of day or shorter sessions to find what works best for you.

Practising Self-Compassion

1. Be Kind to Yourself

Being too hard on yourself after a setback can lead to a negative cycle of guilt and discouragement. Practising self-compassion is crucial for bouncing back.

Anecdote: Lisa missed her habit of practising the piano for a week due to illness. She felt guilty and worried about losing her progress. However, she reminded herself that her health came first and that it was okay to take a break. This self-compassionate approach helped her return to her practice with renewed motivation.

Prescription: Talk to yourself as you would to a friend. Remind yourself that it's okay to have setbacks and that taking a break doesn't mean you've failed.

2. Focus on Progress, Not Perfection

It's easy to get caught up in an all-or-nothing mindset, but focusing on progress rather than perfection can help you stay motivated.

Anecdote: Tom aimed to exercise five times a week but often managed only three. Instead of feeling like a failure, he chose to celebrate the three days he exercised. This shift in perspective kept him motivated and encouraged him to keep going.

Prescription: Celebrate the progress you've made, no matter how small. Every step forward counts, and perfection is not the goal.

3. Practice Gratitude

Gratitude can shift your focus from what went wrong to what's going well. This positive outlook can boost your motivation and resilience.

Anecdote: Emily missed her habit of journaling for a few days due to a busy schedule. Instead of focusing on the missed days, she wrote down things she was grateful for, including the reasons she was busy. This gratitude practice helped her maintain a positive mindset and get back to her journaling habit.

Prescription: Incorporate a gratitude practice into your routine. Reflect on what you're grateful for, especially during setbacks, to maintain a positive outlook.

Building Resilience and Staying Motivated

1. Set Realistic Goals

Setting realistic goals can help you avoid feeling overwhelmed and make it easier to stay on track.

Anecdote: Alex wanted to read more books but found his goal of one book a week too ambitious. He adjusted his goal to one book a month, which felt more achievable and kept him motivated to continue reading.

Prescription: Review your goals and ensure they are realistic and achievable. Adjust them if needed to match your current capacity and circumstances.

2. Create a Support System

Having a support system can provide encouragement and accountability, making it easier to bounce back from setbacks.

Anecdote: David struggled to maintain his new habit of healthy eating. He joined a local nutrition group where members shared recipes and supported each other's goals. The sense of community helped David stay motivated and get back on track after slip-ups.

Prescription: Find a support system, whether it's friends, family or a group with similar goals. Share your journey with them and lean on them for support when needed.

3. Use Reminders and Triggers

Reminders and triggers can help you stay consistent with your habits by keeping them top of mind.

Anecdote: Karen wanted to drink more water but often forgot. She set reminders on her phone and placed water bottles around her home and office. These visual and auditory cues helped her remember to stay hydrated throughout the day.

Prescription: Use reminders and triggers to keep your habits in mind. Set alarms, use sticky notes or create visual cues to prompt you to follow through with your routines.

Staying Flexible and Adapting

1. Be Open to Change

Life is unpredictable, and being open to change can help you stay resilient and motivated.

Anecdote: Michael loved his morning yoga routine but found it challenging to maintain after his work hours changed. Instead of giving up, he adapted by incorporating shorter yoga sessions during his lunch break. This flexibility allowed him to continue his practice despite the change in schedule.

Prescription: Stay open to adapting your habits to fit changing circumstances. Flexibility is critical to maintaining consistency and motivation.

2. Embrace the Journey

Focus on the journey rather than just the destination. Embracing the process can make it more enjoyable and sustainable.

Anecdote: Rachel set a goal to run a marathon but found the training regimen overwhelming. She shifted her focus to enjoying each run and celebrating her progress. This mindset made the journey enjoyable and kept her motivated to continue training.

Prescription: Embrace the journey and find joy in the process.

Celebrate small victories and enjoy the progress you make along the way.

3. Reflect and Adjust Regularly

Regular reflection and adjustment can help you stay aligned with your goals and make necessary changes to your habits.

Anecdote: John reviewed his habit of reading before bed and realized that he often fell asleep after just a few pages. He adjusted by setting aside time to read in the afternoon instead, which worked better with his energy levels and helped him stay consistent.

Prescription: Set aside time for regular reflection on your habits. Identify what's working and what isn't, and make necessary adjustments to stay on track.

Practical Tips for Bouncing Back

Step 1: Acknowledge the Setback

Recognize and acknowledge when you've slipped up without judgement. This is the first step towards bouncing back.

Exercise: Take a few minutes to reflect on the setback. Write down your feelings and thoughts about what happened and why.

Step 2: Reflect and Learn

Understand the cause of the setback and what you can learn from it. Use this insight to make necessary adjustments.

Exercise: Reflect on the circumstances that led to the setback. Identify any patterns or triggers and consider how you can address them in the future.

Step 3: Adjust Your Approach

Make adjustments to your habits or routines based on what you've learned. Flexibility is key to staying consistent.

Exercise: Identify one adjustment you can make to your habit or routine to make it more manageable. Implement this change and observe how it impacts your consistency.

Step 4: Practice Self-Compassion

Be kind to yourself and avoid self-criticism. Remember that setbacks are a normal part of the journey.

Exercise: Write a compassionate letter to yourself as if you were comforting a friend. Acknowledge your efforts and remind yourself that it's okay to have setbacks.

Step 5: Recommit and Move Forward

Recommit to your habit with a renewed sense of purpose. Focus on the progress you've made and the benefits you've experienced.

Exercise: Revisit your goals and remind yourself why you started the habit in the first place. Write down your renewed commitment and the benefits you've experienced.

Real-Life Examples of Bouncing Back

Example 1: Overcoming Fitness Setbacks

Jessica started a new fitness routine with great enthusiasm but sprained her ankle a few weeks in. She felt demotivated and worried about losing her progress. After acknowledging her disappointment, she adjusted her routine to include upper-body workouts and swimming, which didn't strain her ankle. This adjustment allowed her to stay active and bounce back once her ankle healed.

Takeaway: Flexibility and adjustment are crucial when facing setbacks. Find alternative ways to stay on track and maintain your progress.

Example 2: Recommitting to a Writing Habit

Alex set a goal to write daily but found it difficult to maintain during a particularly busy period at work. He felt guilty and considered giving up. However, he acknowledged his frustration, reflected on his schedule and adjusted his writing sessions to shorter, more focused periods. This adjustment made it easier for him to stay consistent and recommit to his writing habit.

Takeaway: Adjusting your approach and setting realistic goals can help you stay committed to your habits, even during busy times.

Example 3: Returning to Healthy Eating

David had been following a healthy eating plan but slipped up during the holidays. He felt demotivated and considered giving up. However, he acknowledged that occasional indulgences were normal, reflected on his overall progress and adjusted his plan to include healthy meals he enjoyed. This self-compassionate approach helped him get back on track and maintain his healthy eating habits.

Takeaway: Self-compassion and reflection can help you bounce back from setbacks and maintain your healthy habits.

Takeaways: Practical Prescriptions for Staying Motivated

1. Acknowledge Your Feelings:

- Recognize and acknowledge your feelings without judgment when you slip up.
- Write down your feelings to help process them and prepare to start again.

2. Reflect on the Cause:
   - Understand why you slipped up and use this insight to make necessary adjustments.
   - Reflect on the circumstances and identify patterns or triggers.

3. Adjust Your Approach:
   - Make adjustments to your habits or routines to make them more manageable.
   - Experiment with different times of day or shorter sessions to find what works best.

4. Be Kind to Yourself:
   - Practice self-compassion and avoid self-criticism. Talk to yourself as you would to a friend.
   - Write a compassionate letter to yourself to acknowledge your efforts and remind yourself it's okay to have setbacks.

5. Focus on Progress, Not Perfection:
   - Celebrate the progress you've made, no matter how small. Every step forward counts.
   - Shift your focus from achieving perfection to making consistent progress.

6. Practice Gratitude:
   - Incorporate a gratitude practice into your routine to maintain a positive outlook.
   - Reflect on what you're grateful for, especially during setbacks.

7. Set Realistic Goals:
   - Review your goals and ensure they are realistic and

achievable. Adjust them if needed.
- Set smaller, more manageable goals to avoid feeling overwhelmed.
8. Create a Support System:
    - Find a support system of friends, family, or groups with similar goals.
    - Share your journey with them and lean on them for encouragement and accountability.
9. Use Reminders and Triggers:
    - Use reminders and triggers to keep your habits in mind. Set alarms or create visual cues.
    - Place reminders in visible locations to prompt you to follow through with your routines.
10. Stay Open to Change:
    - Be open to adapting your habits to fit changing circumstances. Flexibility is key to staying consistent.
    - Embrace the journey and find joy in the process. Celebrate small victories and enjoy the progress you make.
11. Reflect and Adjust Regularly:
    - Set aside time for regular reflection on your habits. Identify what's working and what isn't.
    - Make necessary adjustments to stay aligned with your goals and maintain motivation.

By following these strategies and insights, you'll be well-equipped to stay motivated and bounce back from setbacks.

20

The Journey to Lasting Change: Building Small Habits for a Lifetime

By now, you've learned a lot about habits, motivation and the importance of flexibility. But how do you put all this knowledge into practice? How do you start with small habits, stay focused and consistent, harness the power of repetition and make good habits a permanent part of your life? And how do you adapt your habits to the ever-changing world we live in? Let's dive into these questions and explore practical strategies to help you on your journey to lasting change.

Starting with Small Habits

The Power of Tiny Changes

When it comes to building habits, starting small is key. Tiny changes are easier to manage and less overwhelming, making it more likely that you'll stick with them.

Take Emily, for example. She wanted to build a habit of reading more books but felt daunted by the idea of reading for an hour every day. Instead, she started with just five minutes of reading each night before bed. This tiny habit felt manageable, and over time, she found herself reading for longer periods naturally.

Prescription: Identify a habit you want to develop and break it down into the smallest possible action. Start with that tiny step and gradually build from there.

Example: Tom wanted to incorporate more physical activity into his day but struggled with consistency. He set a goal to do just one push-up every morning. Each time he completed his push-up, he celebrated his success, which motivated him to add more push-ups gradually.

Prescription: Set small, achievable goals and celebrate each success. Recognize and reward yourself for every step forward, no matter how small.

Celebrating Small Wins

Celebrating small wins can boost your motivation and reinforce positive behaviour, making it easier to build and maintain new habits.

Sarah aimed to drink more water daily but often forgot. She decided to start with a single glass of water first thing in the morning. Each day she successfully drank her morning glass, she gave herself a mental pat on the back. This small win motivated her to gradually increase her water intake throughout the day.

Prescription: Set incremental goals that are easy to achieve and celebrate each one. These small victories build confidence and encourage further progress.

Example: James wanted to improve his diet but found it hard to give up his favourite unhealthy snacks. He decided to start by adding a piece of fruit to his breakfast every day. Over time, this small change led to healthier eating habits overall.

Prescription: Introduce small, positive changes to your routine and acknowledge the effort you're putting in. Small adjustments can lead to significant improvements over time.

Staying Focused and Consistent

The Role of Focus

Staying focused is crucial for habit formation. Distractions can derail your progress, so it's important to create an environment that supports your new habits.

Sarah wanted to build a habit of writing daily but found herself easily distracted by her phone. She decided to create a dedicated writing space free from distractions. By removing her phone and other potential interruptions, she was able to stay focused and consistent with her writing habit.

Prescription: Identify potential distractions and find ways to minimize them. Create a dedicated space and time for your new habit to help you stay focused.

Example: Michael wanted to study more effectively but kept getting distracted by his noisy household. He found a quiet corner in the local library where he could study undisturbed. This change in environment helped him concentrate better and stick to his study schedule.

Prescription: Evaluate your environment and make necessary changes to minimize distractions. A dedicated space can significantly enhance your ability to stay focused.

Building a Routine

Consistency is key to turning a new habit into a lasting one. Building a routine around your habit can make it a regular part of your day.

David wanted to meditate daily but struggled to find the time. He decided to pair his meditation habit with his morning coffee. Each day, after brewing his coffee, he spent five minutes meditating. This routine helped him stay consistent and made meditation a regular part of his morning.

Prescription: Pair your new habit with an existing routine or daily activity. This practice, known as habit stacking, can help you integrate the new habit into your daily life more easily.

Example: Jessica wanted to exercise regularly but found it hard to make time in the evenings. She decided to incorporate a short workout into her morning routine right after brushing her teeth. This small change helped her establish a consistent exercise habit.

Prescription: Identify a current habit and stack a new habit onto it. This strategy leverages existing routines to build new, consistent behaviours.

The Power of Repetition

How Repetition Reinforces Habits

Repetition is the backbone of habit formation. The more you repeat a behaviour, the more it becomes ingrained in your brain, eventually turning into an automatic action.

Mark wanted to build a habit of flossing daily. Initially, he found it hard to remember, but by consistently flossing every night after brushing his teeth, the action became automatic. Now, he doesn't even think about it; flossing is just part of his nightly routine.

Prescription: Commit to repeating your new habit regularly, even if it feels tedious at first. With time and repetition, it will become second nature.

Example: Emily aimed to journal every evening but often forgot. She set a reminder on her phone for the same time each night. After several weeks of journaling at the same time, it became a natural part of her evening routine.

Prescription: Use reminders and consistent timing to help reinforce your habit. Regular repetition at the same time each day can solidify the behaviour.

Tracking Your Progress

Keeping track of your progress can help you stay motivated and see how far you've come. It also reinforces the habit through consistent repetition.

Emma used a habit-tracking app to monitor her daily exercise. Seeing her progress visualized in the app motivated her to stay consistent and kept her accountable.

Prescription: Use a habit-tracking app or a simple journal to record your progress. Check off each day you complete your habit and watch your streak grow.

Example: Robert wanted to improve his language skills and set a goal to practice Spanish daily. He used a calendar to mark off each day he practiced. The visual representation of his progress motivated him to continue his streak.

Prescription: Keep a visual record of your habit progress. Seeing your consistency can motivate you to keep going and not break the chain.

Staying Motivated

Finding Your Why

Understanding why you want to build a habit can provide a powerful source of motivation. Connecting with your deeper purpose can keep you going even when things get tough.

John wanted to quit smoking but struggled with motivation. He reflected on his reasons for quitting and realized that his primary motivation was to be healthier for his young children. This deeper purpose gave him the strength to stay committed to his goal.

Prescription: Reflect on your reasons for wanting to build a new habit. Write them down and revisit them regularly to remind yourself of your deeper purpose.

Example: Lisa wanted to run a marathon but found the training grueling. She reminded herself of her goal to raise awareness and funds for a charity close to her heart. This purpose kept her motivated during tough training sessions.

Prescription: Identify a deeper purpose behind your habit. Connecting your actions to a larger goal can provide lasting motivation.

Using Positive Reinforcement

Positive reinforcement can boost your motivation and help you stay committed to your habits. Rewarding yourself for your efforts reinforces positive behaviour.

Lisa set a goal to walk 10,000 steps daily. She rewarded herself with a relaxing bath and her favourite book each time she hit her goal. These rewards made the habit more enjoyable and kept her motivated.

Prescription: Identify rewards that will motivate you and use them to reinforce your habits. Make sure the rewards are meaningful and enjoyable.

Example: Karen aimed to save money each month but struggled with impulse purchases. She set a reward for herself: each month she successfully saved, she allowed herself to buy a small treat. This positive reinforcement helped her stay on track.

Prescription: Choose rewards that align with your goals and motivate you to stay consistent. Celebrate your successes to reinforce positive habits.

Avoiding Bad Habits and Reinforcing Good Ones

Identifying Triggers

Understanding what triggers your bad habits can help you avoid them. By identifying and addressing these triggers, you can create an environment that supports your good habits.

Karen realized that she reached for junk food whenever she felt stressed. By identifying stress as her trigger, she started practicing deep breathing exercises and keeping healthy snacks on hand. This change helped her avoid junk food and reinforce healthier eating habits.

Prescription: Reflect on what triggers your bad habits and find healthier alternatives to address those triggers. Create an environment that supports your good habits.

Example: Tom noticed he often procrastinated on work tasks by browsing social media. He identified boredom as the trigger and started taking short breaks to walk or stretch instead. This helped him reduce procrastination and stay focused on his tasks.

Prescription: Identify the triggers for your bad habits and replace them with healthier actions. Create strategies to manage these triggers effectively.

Building a Support System

Having a support system can provide encouragement and accountability, helping you avoid bad habits and stay committed to good ones.

Alex wanted to cut back on drinking but found it challenging to do it alone. He joined a support group where members shared their experiences and supported each other's goals. The sense of community helped Alex stay committed to his goal.

Prescription: Find a support system, whether it's friends, family or a group with similar goals. Share your journey with them and lean on them for support and encouragement.

Example: Emily wanted to wake up earlier but struggled with consistency. She partnered with a friend who had the same goal, and they held each other accountable by checking in every morning. This mutual support helped them both succeed.

Prescription: Partner with someone who shares your goal. Mutual accountability can provide motivation and support to help you stay on track.

Making Good Habits Part of Your Life

Integrating Habits into Your Identity

When you start to see your habits as part of your identity, they become more ingrained in your life. This shift in perspective can make it easier to maintain good habits in the long term.

Emily wanted to become more active. Instead of seeing exercise as a chore, she started identifying as someone who enjoys being active. This mindset shift made it easier for her to integrate exercise into her daily life and maintain her fitness habits.

Prescription: Start thinking of yourself as the type of person who embodies your desired habits. For example, if you want to read more, see yourself as a reader. This identity shift can reinforce your habits.

Example: Michael wanted to eat healthier but found it hard to resist unhealthy foods. He started identifying as a health-conscious person and made choices that aligned with this new identity. Over time, healthy eating became a natural part of his life.

Prescription: Embrace the identity associated with your habit. Seeing yourself as the type of person who practises the habit can reinforce your commitment.

Staying Flexible and Adapting to Change

Life is constantly changing, and being able to adapt your habits to new circumstances is crucial for maintaining them long-term.

David had a habit of going to the gym every evening, but when his work hours changed, he found it challenging to keep up. Instead of giving up, he adapted by incorporating home workouts and morning runs. This flexibility allowed him to stay active despite the change in his schedule.

Prescription: Stay open to adjusting your habits to fit changing circumstances. Flexibility is key to maintaining consistency and motivation.

Example: Karen loved her evening yoga classes but had to relocate for work. She adapted by finding online yoga sessions that fit her new schedule. This flexibility helped her maintain her practice despite the change.

Prescription: Be willing to adjust your habits as needed. Flexibility ensures that you can maintain your habits even when circumstances change.

Real-Life Examples and Anecdotes

Example 1: Overcoming Procrastination

Rachel struggled with procrastination when it came to her schoolwork. She decided to start with just five minutes of study time each day. This small, manageable habit helped her overcome the initial resistance, and over time, she found herself studying for longer periods naturally.

Takeaway: Starting small can help you overcome resistance and build consistency. Celebrate each small win to stay motivated.

Example 2: Building a Healthy Eating Habit

Tom wanted to eat healthier but found it challenging to give up his favourite junk foods. He started by adding one healthy meal to his diet each day. This gradual approach made the transition easier, and over time, he found himself craving healthier foods.

Takeaway: Gradual changes are more sustainable than drastic ones. Focus on adding positive habits rather than eliminating negative ones entirely.

Example 3: Staying Active with a Busy Schedule

Emily had a demanding job that left her with little time for exercise. She started doing short, high-intensity workouts during her lunch breaks. These quick sessions fit into her busy schedule and kept her active.

Takeaway: Find creative ways to integrate habits into your existing routine. Even short sessions can make a big difference.

Example 4: Adapting to New Circumstances

Mark enjoyed running but faced challenges when he moved to a city with harsh winters. Instead of giving up, he adapted by joining an indoor running club and incorporating strength training. This flexibility allowed him to stay consistent with his fitness goals.

Takeaway: Flexibility and adaptability are crucial for maintaining habits in changing circumstances. Be open to trying new approaches.

Takeaways: Practical Prescriptions for Lasting Change

1. Start Small:
   - Identify the smallest possible action you can take to build a new habit.
   - Celebrate each small win to boost your motivation.
2. Stay Focused and Consistent:
   - Minimize distractions and create a dedicated space for your habit.
   - Pair your new habit with an existing routine to build consistency.
3. Harness the Power of Repetition:
   - Commit to repeating your new habit regularly, even if it feels tedious at first.
   - Use reminders and consistent timing to reinforce the behaviour.
4. Track Your Progress:
   - Keep a visual record of your habit progress, such as a journal or habit-tracking app.

- Seeing your consistency can motivate you to keep going.
5. Find Your Why:
    - Reflect on your reasons for wanting to build a new habit and write them down.
    - Revisit your reasons regularly to remind yourself of your deeper purpose.
6. Use Positive Reinforcement:
    - Identify rewards that will motivate you and use them to reinforce your habits.
    - Choose rewards that align with your goals and celebrate your successes.
7. Identify and Address Triggers:
    - Reflect on what triggers your bad habits and find healthier alternatives to address those triggers.
    - Create an environment that supports your good habits.
8. Build a Support System:
    - Find a support system, whether it's friends, family or a group with similar goals.
    - Share your journey with them and lean on them for support and encouragement.
9. Integrate Habits into Your Identity:
    - Start thinking of yourself as the type of person who embodies your desired habits.
    - Embrace the identity associated with your habit to reinforce your commitment.
10. Stay Flexible and Adapt:
    - Be open to adjusting your habits to fit changing circumstances.
    - Flexibility ensures that you can maintain your habits even when circumstances change.

21

To Establish New Routines, Learn to Embrace Setbacks

No one ever gets out of bed on 1 January vowing, "This is going to be the year I fail!" Maybe we ought to, though.

The key to breaking bad habits is mastering the art of breaking good ones. According to Dr Christine Carter, a sociologist, being willing to be awful at anything at first is crucial if we want to successfully adopt a new habit. New habits, or any worthwhile habits, will feel awkward at first, regardless of how intelligent or talented we are. It is more probable that we will stumble than that we will reach a state of flow instantly. We must learn to fall short in baby steps because our thoughts will always want to keep us from that result.

Here are four methods I teach in my workshops that have helped many of my clients establish new habits that last longer than a week or two and eventually become second nature.

Protect yourself from major disappointments

When the sale fell through, business tycoon Jia Jiang was revelling in his recent acquisition. Even though he understood it was a talent he'd need as an entrepreneur, he detested being rejected. In order to strengthen his resistance to rejection, Jiang devised a 100-day set of controlled tests in which he would encounter the word "no" frequently. These varied from requesting to play football in someone's backyard to requesting to give the weather report during a live TV interview.

Experiments where you will fail little but often can protect you from major disappointments. Abhor being on camera? You seem increasingly anxious as you speak, and your voice trembles and you fumble over your words. Minimise the size of your experiments. In a meeting when you aren't required to speak up, record yourself saying a single sentence and watch the film afterwards. Another option is to pose a single question out loud. We can lessen the impact of failure and increase the likelihood of success by gradually exposing ourselves to the strength we are aiming to develop. As we progress through the steps, our resilience to the challenges of a new habit grows, which in turn increases our likelihood of success down the road.

Prevent yourself from giving in by committing

We are both excited and terrified of falling short of our lofty ambitions. Whether it's writing that strategy document or having that tough talk, we're quick to tell ourselves that today isn't the right day to begin. However, there is a sliver of time between envisioning our end state and the moment when our instincts tell us to back down. Make a promise to another person during this window. Saying something like, "I'd like to discuss our approach to design," might help you have an honest conversation with a coworker. Would next week work for you? Even if you don't want to start the project just yet, you should nonetheless write the email that will accompany the intimidating deliverable. We can get out of our minds and hold ourselves responsible to another person by starting with an email. Retracting a declaration

Make known the things you've discovered

Getting back up after a fall is more important than falling at all, as the old adage goes. Similarly, when you have minor setbacks, reflect on what you've learnt. When we haven't found the magic formula, we try to stay out of the spotlight (and maybe even take a sick day or two). To counteract the humiliation of failing, you should instead emphasize the benefits of learning.

A "lessons learned" database is one feature of the company where I am employed. Team members add to this repository after each milestone by reflecting on what they learnt. After reviewing these findings, colleagues working on the subsequent project can go to work. At the individual level, you can take stock of what you've learned, write it down or present it to your team in a meeting; either way, you'll always have it on hand. Furthermore, while you are learning new skills, it is best to start with more cautious terminology. You can put yourself in the perspective of a learner by framing something as an experiment, beta or draft. You can move faster, get useful input and gain buy-in without worrying about being perfect.

Remind yourself to take breaks and maintain a progress metre.

If we want to get from couch to marathon, we shouldn't punish ourselves every time we skip a run. Our motivation to keep going gets eroded every time we hold ourselves responsible or shame ourselves. Rather of evaluating each day independently, track focuses on the big picture. You can see your progress over time by maintaining a record of your efforts. Also, don't keep going when you're not enjoying or performing well enough with your new habit. Set a time limit and don't go over it, or look back at your performance from the previous days to see when your mood goes from pumped to deflated. That way, you'll know when to quit before your performance goes downhill. Instead of being down over a B performance, you'll be looking forward to the next session with glee.

Even while our habits and thoughts beg us to dream big, we never really do because we're always afraid we won't measure up. Achieving long-term transformation begins with dipping our toes into small-scale failure. When there isn't a high risk of failure and a high potential reward, it's easier to change habits.

22

Interactive Exercises for Forming Good Habits

Welcome to this interactive chapter! Here, we'll put what you've learned into practice through exercises, questions and activities designed to help you form good habits, identify and avoid bad habits, and track your progress. Get ready to engage, reflect and take actionable steps towards lasting change.

Exercise 1: Reflecting on Your Current Habits

Before you can form new habits, it's essential to understand your current ones. This exercise will help you identify your existing habits and evaluate their impact on your life.

Instructions:

1. List Your Daily Habits:
- Take a moment to write down all the habits you currently have, both good and bad. Be honest and thorough.

Example:
- Good Habits: Morning exercise, reading before bed, drinking water.
- Bad Habits: Procrastinating on work, excessive screen time, late-night snacking.

2. Evaluate Each Habit:
- For each habit, ask yourself the following questions:
- How does this habit make me feel?
- What are the short-term and long-term effects of this habit?
- Does this habit align with my goals and values?

Reflection:
- Write down your thoughts and feelings about each habit. This reflection will help you understand which habits are beneficial and which ones you might want to change.

Exercise 2: Setting Small, Achievable Goals

To build new habits, start small. This exercise will guide you in setting achievable goals and creating a plan to incorporate them into your daily routine.

Instructions:

1. Identify a New Habit:
- Choose one new habit you want to develop. It should be something small and manageable.

Example:
- New Habit: Drinking a glass of water first thing in the morning.

2. Set a Specific Goal:
- Make your goal specific, measurable and time-bound.

Example:
- Goal: Drink one glass of water every morning for the next 30 days.

3. Create a Plan:
- Outline the steps you need to take to achieve your goal.

Consider what time of day you'll perform the habit, any tools you need and potential obstacles.

Example:
- Plan: Keep a glass of water by my bedside table. Set a reminder on my phone to drink the water as soon as I wake up.

4. Track Your Progress:
- Use a habit tracker or journal to record your progress. Check off each day you successfully complete your habit.

Exercise 3: Understanding and Avoiding Bad Habits

Bad habits can be tricky to break. This exercise will help you identify your bad habits and create strategies to avoid them.

Instructions:

1. Identify Bad Habits:
- Write down the bad habits you want to address.

Example:
- Bad Habit: Procrastinating on work.

2. Analyze Triggers:
- For each bad habit, identify the triggers that lead to the behaviour. Triggers could be emotions, environments or specific situations.

Example:
- Trigger: Feeling overwhelmed by large tasks.

3. Develop Alternatives:
- Think of healthier alternatives to replace your bad habits. These should be actions that address the same triggers but in a positive way.

Example:
- Alternative: Break down large tasks into smaller, manageable steps and start with the easiest one.

4. Create an Action Plan:
- Write down your action plan to avoid the bad habit and implement the alternative behaviour.

Example:
- Action Plan: When feeling overwhelmed, take a deep breath, list the steps needed for the task and start with the simplest one.

Exercise 4: Using Positive Reinforcement

Positive reinforcement can help you stay motivated and committed to your new habits. This exercise will guide you in setting up a reward system.

Instructions:

1. Choose a Habit to Reinforce:
- Select a habit you want to strengthen with positive reinforcement.

Example:
- Habit: Exercising three times a week.

2. Identify Meaningful Rewards:
- Think of rewards that are meaningful and enjoyable for you. They should be something you look forward to but that you only get if you complete the habit.

Example:
- Rewards: A relaxing bath, a movie night, a favourite snack.

3. Set Up a Reward System:
- Decide how often you'll reward yourself and what the criteria will be.

Example:
- Reward System: For every week that I exercise three times, I'll treat myself to a movie night on Saturday.

4. Track Your Progress:
- Keep a record of your habit completion and reward yourself accordingly. Reflect on how the rewards impact your motivation.

Exercise 5: Creating a Support System

A strong support system can provide encouragement and accountability. This exercise will help you build a network of support for your habit goals.

Instructions:

1. Identify Your Support Network:
- Write down the names of people who can support you in your habit goals. These could be friends, family members, colleagues or support groups.

Example:
- Support Network: My best friend, my partner, my coworker an online fitness group.

2. Communicate Your Goals:
- Share your habit goals with your support network. Be specific about what you're trying to achieve and how they can help.

Example:
- Communication: "I'm trying to exercise three times a week.

Can you help by checking in with me on my progress and encouraging me to stick with it?"

3. Set Up Regular Check-Ins:
- Schedule regular check-ins with your support network to discuss your progress and any challenges you're facing.

Example:
- Check-Ins: Weekly coffee chats with my best friend to talk about our fitness goals.

4. Offer and Seek Encouragement:
- Encourage mutual support by offering to help others with their habit goals as well.

Example:
- Encouragement: "Let's motivate each other to stay on track. I'll cheer you on with your goals, and you do the same for me."

Exercise 6: Reflecting on Progress and Adjusting Goals

Regular reflection and adjustment can help you stay on track and make necessary changes to your habits. This exercise will guide you in reflecting on your progress and setting new goals.

Instructions:

1. Reflect on Your Progress:
- Take time to reflect on your habit journey so far. Consider what's working, what's not and why.

Example Questions:
- What habits have I successfully built?
- What challenges have I faced?
- How do I feel about my progress?

2. Identify Areas for Improvement:
- Based on your reflection, identify areas where you can improve or make adjustments.

Example:
- Area for Improvement: I've struggled to stick with my reading habit because I get too tired at night. I could try reading in the morning instead.

3. Set New Goals:
- Set new, specific goals based on your reflection. These could be adjustments to existing habits or new habits you want to develop.

Example:
- New Goal: Read for 10 minutes every morning after breakfast.

4. Create an Action Plan:
- Outline the steps you need to take to achieve your new goals. Consider potential obstacles and how you'll address them.

Example:
- Action Plan: Set a reminder on my phone to read after breakfast. Keep my book on the kitchen table so it's easy to access.

Exercise 7: Tracking Your Habits

Tracking your habits can help you stay accountable and motivated. This exercise will guide you in setting up a habit tracking system.

Instructions:

1. Choose Your Tracking Method:
- Decide how you want to track your habits. Options include a journal, a calendar or a habit-tracking app.

Example:
- Tracking Method: A habit-tracking app that lets me check off each day I complete my habit.

2. List Your Habits:
- Write down the habits you want to track. Be specific about the behaviour you're tracking.

Example:
- Habits: Drink a glass of water each morning, exercise three times a week and read for 10 minutes each day.

3. Set Up Your Tracker:
- Set up your chosen tracking method with your habits. Make sure it's easy to use and access.

Example:
- Tracker Setup: Enter my habits into the app and set daily reminders to check my progress.

4. Review and Reflect:
- Regularly review your habit tracker and reflect on your progress. Adjust your goals and strategies as needed.

Example Questions:
- How consistent have I been with my habits?
- What patterns do I notice?
- What adjustments can I make to improve?

Exercise 8: Adapting to Change

Life is constantly changing, and being able to adapt your habits to new circumstances is crucial for maintaining them long-term. This exercise will help you stay flexible and adjust your habits as needed.

Instructions:

1. Identify Potential Changes:
- Think about upcoming changes in your life that might impact your habits. These could be changes in your schedule, environment or responsibilities.

Example:
- Potential Change: Starting a new job with longer hours.

2. Plan for Adjustments:
- Consider how you can adjust your habits to fit these changes. Be flexible and open to trying new approaches.

Example:
- Adjustment Plan: If I have longer work hours, I can switch my exercise routine to shorter, more intense workouts in the morning.

3. Stay Flexible:
- Be willing to experiment and make changes as needed. Flexibility is key to maintaining consistency and motivation.

Example:
- Flexibility: If my new exercise routine isn't working, I'll try incorporating physical activity into my commute, like biking or walking.

4. Reflect and Reevaluate:
- Regularly reflect on how your habits are fitting into your new circumstances. Adjust your goals and strategies as needed.

Example Questions:
- How are my habits fitting into my new routine?
- What adjustments can I make to improve my consistency?
- How do I feel about my progress?

Exercise 9: Using Visualization and Affirmations

Visualization and affirmations can boost your motivation and help you stay committed to your habits. This exercise will guide you in using these techniques effectively.

Instructions:

1. Visualize Success:
- Spend a few minutes each day visualizing yourself successfully completing your habits. Imagine how it feels and the positive impact it has on your life.

Example:
- Visualization: Picture yourself finishing a workout feeling strong and energized, or completing a study session feeling accomplished and prepared.

2. Create Affirmations:
- Write down positive affirmations that reinforce your commitment to your habits. Repeat them daily to boost your motivation.

Example:
- Affirmations: "I am committed to my health and fitness." "I am a focused and dedicated student." "I make choices that support my well-being."

3. Incorporate Visualization and Affirmations into Your Routine:
- Find a time each day to practice visualization and affirmations. This could be in the morning, before bed or during a break.

Example:
- Routine: Spend five minutes each morning visualizing your success and repeating your affirmations.

4. Reflect on the Impact:
- Reflect on how visualization and affirmations impact your motivation and consistency. Adjust your practice as needed.

Example Questions:
- How do I feel after practicing visualization and affirmations?
- Have these practices boosted my motivation and commitment?
- What adjustments can I make to improve their effectiveness?

Exercise 10: Creating a Long-Term Vision

Having a long-term vision can help you stay focused and motivated. This exercise will guide you in creating a vision for your habits and goals.

Instructions:

1. Identify Your Long-Term Goals:
- Think about what you want to achieve in the long term. Write down your goals and the habits that will help you reach them.

Example:
- Long-Term Goals: Run a marathon, graduate with honors, build a successful business.

2. Create a Vision Board:
- Create a vision board that represents your long-term goals and habits. Use images, words and quotes that inspire you.

Example:
- Vision Board: Include pictures of marathon runners, motivational quotes about perseverance and images representing academic success.

3. Outline a Plan:
- Outline a plan for how you'll achieve your long-term goals. Break them down into smaller, actionable steps.

Example:
- Plan: For running a marathon, start with a 5K training plan, then progress to 10K, half marathon, and finally marathon training.

4. Review and Adjust:
- Regularly review your vision board and plan. Reflect on your progress and adjust your goals and strategies as needed.

Example Questions:
- Am I making progress toward my long-term goals?
- What adjustments can I make to stay on track?
- How do I feel about my progress?

Conclusion

By engaging in these exercises, you've taken significant steps toward building and maintaining good habits, identifying and avoiding bad habits and staying motivated and adaptable. Remember, habit formation is a journey, and it's essential to stay flexible, reflect regularly and celebrate your progress. Keep using these exercises to guide your journey and continue growing and evolving. Happy habit-forming!

Takeaways: Practical Prescriptions for Lasting Change

1. Start Small:
   - Begin with the smallest possible action to build a new habit.
   - Celebrate each small win to boost your motivation.

2. Stay Focused and Consistent:
   - Minimize distractions and create a dedicated space for your habit.
   - Pair your new habit with an existing routine to build consistency.
3. Harness the Power of Repetition:
   - Commit to repeating your new habit regularly, even if it feels tedious at first.
   - Use reminders and consistent timing to reinforce the behaviour.
4. Track Your Progress:
   - Keep a visual record of your habit progress, such as a journal or habit-tracking app.
   - Seeing your consistency can motivate you to keep going.
5. Find Your Why:
   - Reflect on your reasons for wanting to build a new habit and write them down.
   - Revisit your reasons regularly to remind yourself of your deeper purpose.
6. Use Positive Reinforcement:
   - Identify rewards that will motivate you and use them to reinforce your habits.
   - Choose rewards that align with your goals and celebrate your successes.
7. Identify and Address Triggers:
   - Reflect on what triggers your bad habits and find healthier alternatives to address those triggers.
   - Create an environment that supports your good habits.

Happy habit-forming!

www.ingramcontent.com/pod-product-compliance
Lightning Source LLC
Chambersburg PA
CBHW032127160426
43197CB00008B/543